Faith and Culture

A Multicultural Catechetical Resource

**Department of Education
United States Catholic Conference**

In its planning document, as approved by the general membership of the United States Catholic Conference in November 1985, the Department of Education and its Desk of Special Catechetical Projects were authorized to produce a practical catechetical resource that would support and foster multicultural catechesis within the Church in the United States. This present publication, *Faith and Culture: A Multicultural Catechetical Resource,* has been approved by Rev. Thomas G. Gallagher, Secretary of Education, and authorized for publication by the undersigned.

Monsignor Daniel F. Hoye
General Secretary
NCCB/USCC

February 4, 1987

Typefaces: Caslon and Antique Olive
Typography: World Composition Services, Inc.
        Leesburg, Va.

ISBN 1-55586-994-7

Contents

Foreword

"Christ, in the members of his Body, is himself African. . . . The Church is to be fully African and fully Christian."

Those words of Pope John Paul II, addressed to the peoples of Africa, are a statement to the universal Church about the entire catechetical enterprise. This striking exclamation tells us that Christ and his teachings must be appropriated by particular ethnic communities in such a way that the language and culture of the people are employed in explaining and passing on the faith. Also, Pope Paul VI, in *Evangelii Nuntiandi*, noted: ". . . the kingdom which the Gospel proclaims is lived by men who are profoundly linked to a culture, and the building up of the kingdom cannot avoid borrowing the elements of human culture or cultures."

In *Faith and Culture: A Multicultural Catechetical Resource*, the bishops of the United States respond to the many exhortations of the pope to give a truly pastoral flavor to the art of catechesis and to the task of making the Scriptures and tradition intelligible to the Christian faithful. This catechetical inculturation is particularly necessary in the United States, a country of numerous and diverse peoples of various racial, ethnic, and cultural backgrounds.

All who read this book shall find a solid theological foundation for their efforts to bring the good news to our African American, Asian, Hispanic, and native American peoples. Further, the reader shall discover the rich contributions that these peoples offer to the Church.

A sixth-century unknown father of the Church once said, "As individuals who received the Holy Spirit in those days could speak in all kinds of tongues, so today, the Church, united by the Holy Spirit, speaks in the language to every people."

May this same Holy Spirit infuse us with the one language of love that enables us to see in all people the God in whose image we have been created.

Most Rev. James P. Lyke, OFM
Auxiliary Bishop of Cleveland

1

Introduction

The universal Church is one family comprised of persons of many cultures. The Church in the United States is a microcosm of this universal Church. In *Sharing the Light of Faith: National Catechetical Directory for Catholics of the United States,* the bishops remind us that "through catechesis, all should be encouraged to know and respect other cultural, racial, and ethnic groups" (NCD, 181). This is one of the major catechetical opportunities and challenges of the Church in the United States.

Every person is a story of God; so too is every race, culture, and ethnic group. Each one is a gift shared by God in our midst that calls us as catechists and evangelists to a commitment of conversion—to evangelize and to be evangelized. It is like Paul, who being aware of the Hellenistic gods, could share his "unknown" God with the Gentiles. It is like Paul, who was bilingual and multicultural. At times, he even had difficulty in dealing with the misunderstanding of the Jewish community on his ministry to the Gentiles.

Multicultural catechesis is an educational process that links the relationships between the message of salvation and human culture. Multicultural catechesis responds to the Church's mandate to evangelize culture and cultures, not superficially but in the full manifestation of the Incarnation (*Gaudium et Spes,* 58–59).

It is in the Incarnation that faith transcends human culture and cultures converting us as a family of believers in One Faith, One Baptism and the Roman Apostolic Church. Regardless that faith transcend cultures, the Church, vigilant of the evangelical values in respecting each person's dignity and gifts, reminds us:

> . . . bring the power of the Gospel into the very heart of culture and cultures. For this purpose, catechesis will seek to know these cultures and their essential components; it will learn their most significant expressions; it will respect their particular values and riches. In this manner, it will be able to offer these cultures the knowledge of the hidden mystery and help them to bring forth from

3

their own living tradition original expressions of Christian life, celebration and thought (*Catechesi Tradendae*, 53).

Therefore, the use of language from a particular ethnic group in the catechetical ministry does not create a "separate church." On the contrary, it responds to full share of the Kingdom of God.

The catechist is called to venture into the inner experience of faith and culture of the catechized without feeling complacent about this new understanding, since it is God's unfolding mystery that is revealed to the catechist by the process of learning and sharing in the story of the catechized. It is ministering to them and allowing them to minister to us. Consequently, the richness of diversities ought not to be feared by us, but rather they should give us the opportunity to share faith, human experience, and development.

It is for reasons such as these that *Faith and Culture: A Multicultural Catechetical Resource* was prepared. Also, to a large extent, this book is the result of the ministry and dedication of my predecessors, Dr. Marina Herrera and Mr. Francisco Diana. Their dedicated ministry has inspired me with the idea of building multicultural bridges in the catechetical ministry. The cultural and religious practices of the people catechized must be reverenced and respected as the roots from which growth in faith occurs.

Faith and Culture is divided into four sections: Theoretical Foundations; Leadership Development; Program Development; and Resources. These sections contain articles written by catechists from the black Catholic community, the Hispanic Catholic community, the native American Catholic community, and the Southeast Asian Catholic community.

It is hoped that this book will assist catechists and Catholic educators to understand better the relationship between faith and culture in their ministry and, thus, enable them to incorporate this relationship into the catechetical programs in their dioceses and parishes. I would like to thank the USCC Office of Publishing and Promotion Services and all the contributors who made *Faith and Culture* possible. I deeply appreciate the support and encouragement of my colleagues within the Department of Education, in particular, Rev. Thomas G. Gallagher, Secretary for Education, for his visionary wisdom on multicultural catechesis.

Armantina R. Pelaez
Staff Assistant for Catechetical Ministry
Department of Education
United States Catholic Conference

I. THEORETICAL FOUNDATIONS

Theoretical Foundations for Multicultural Catechesis
Marina Herrera, Ph.D.

Native American Catechesis and the Ministry of the Word
Rev. Michael Galvan

Cultural and Religious Practices of the Southeast Asian People
Rev. Umberto Nespolo, OMI

Theoretical Foundations for Multicultural Catechesis

Marina Herrera, Ph.D.

An essay on the theoretical foundations for multicultural catechesis does not imply that we are embarking on a new and separate catechetical endeavor needing justification and validation. It implies, however, that the new understanding of our multicultural society with its complex communicational and interrelational dynamics be taken into account as we proclaim the Christian message so that the faith may be made "living, conscious, and active"[1] among ever-widening circles.

This essay has a twofold purpose: to provide those engaged in proclaiming the good news in our multicultural society with a brief historical dimension that will deepen understanding and help clarify the issues; and to articulate insights derived from the biblical, theological, and communication fields that support multicultural catechesis as an approach deserving the attention and the contributions of all those engaged in the catechetical ministry of the churches.

When Did Multicultural Catechesis Begin?

Multicultural catechesis is a direct descendant of the efforts of minorities in the 1960s to highlight the shortcomings of educational systems that consistently stereotyped, distorted, or ignored the contributions of different races and cultures to the life and history of the United States in particular, and to the human quest in general. However, the efforts of secular educators were not easily translatable into religious education language and goals. In those days, religious educators liked to think that the

---

1. Vatican Council II, *Decree on the Pastoral Office of Bishops in the Church*, no. 14.

7

message they proclaimed was not bound to culture and politics and that the content of the message was not to be changed by the demands of minorities to have their contributions recognized.

Most catechetical material of those years left out any or all references to ethnicity and to races not of the Northern European kind. Even the particular cultural and geographical milieu in which saints of the Third World had gained their holiness were ignored or played down in many classrooms. Many of the most noted local Marian devotions around the world received little or no attention. They were replaced instead by the study of Marian titles found in the Litany of Mary (i.e., Immaculate Conception, Seat of Wisdom, etc.). Few American Catholics know, for example, that Our Lady of Guadalupe is the Patroness of the Americas, while every Catholic in the United States knows that St. Patrick is the patron saint of Ireland.

This general disinterest in the religious contributions of groups outside the Northern European traditions was widespread; it pervaded textbooks, programs, and teacher preparation and was concretely reflected in the setting of goals and policies at all levels, from the parish upward. In the late 1970s, it was still easy to find religious materials for children with clearly anti-Hispanic and anti-native American references, even though black faces had begun to appear in the increasingly visual materials of those years.

A book introducing the Psalms to little children, for example, pictured on one page children clearly dressed in the attire of native Americans as the enemies of the white child in the foreground. Because the Lord destroys the enemy (Ps 92:9), the native American children appeared dead on the ground on the following page! When some religious educators wrote to the publisher, he was amazed that no one in his publishing house through whose hands the material had passed had questioned the drawings as inappropriate or biased. He acknowledged the mistake and halted sales of the book until those pages had been revised. Another publication presented all the inhabitants of Central and South America as savages living in caves until the Catholic missionaries arrived. These distortions of historical fact seemed intended to stress the superiority of European Christian culture and peoples. These books are still in circulation, unrevised.

While these distortions are not the norm, they point to the cultural bias of religious educators, publishers, and users of religious materials. This bias is born of what has been a prevailing ethnocentric mentality in the Church and in the society-at-large.

This all-pervasive ethnocentric mentality received its first official and indirect condemnation in *Sharing the Light of Faith: The National Catechetical Directory for Catholics of the United States* (1977). The Directory recognizes that the Church often fostered and protected the ethnic groups; but that "local churches did, at times, fail to appreciate, refuse to try to understand,

and neglected to welcome the newcomers" (NCD, 13). To obviate this situation, the Directory recommends that the needs of cultural, racial, and ethnic groups be taken into account when planning liturgical celebrations and catechetical programs. But the place in which these suggestions appear—within sections dealing with catechesis and liturgies for children, the handicapped, and the elderly—is unfortunate. It reveals a perception within the Church of ethnic groups as being primarily persons with needs, not gifts that can enrich and enhance the entire community of faith. However, a great first step was taken in calling attention to the unique needs of ethnic and racial groups and with the call "to provide funds, research, materials, and personnel for catechesis directed to minority groups" (NCD, 194).

What Is Multicultural Catechesis?

I shy from defining multicultural catechesis. Rather, I prefer to regard it as an educational process by which the Church seeks to incorporate and make active, for the sake of building community, the gifts of faith and the talents of all the Catholic ethnic groups that make their home in the United States. This incorporation takes place through improved multicultural communication, collaboration, and celebration that seek to have both ethnic groups and mainstream groups come into close contact with each other to exchange gifts and to build new patterns of relating and symbolizing our common faith experience.[2]

The first step in this process of education is suggested by the NCD when it states: "Even in culturally homogenous areas and parishes, catechesis should be multicultural in the sense that all should be educated to know and respect other cultural, racial, and ethnic groups" (NCD, 194). Without this basic respect for the dignity, value, and uniqueness of each person, regardless of race, culture, educational attainment, or economic power, all attempts to do multicultural catechesis will fall short of the desired community-building goal.

In the normal processes of creating change, the first step is to have a vision or a goal. In this instance, however, such a goal or vision cannot be created because, for the most part, members of many ethnic groups are not fully incorporated into the life of the Church in this country. They, therefore, have no means of participating in the articulation of a vision of community that takes their gifts, hopes, and aspirations into account. This is because these groups, non-English speaking for the most part, do not

---

2. Cf. Marina Herrera, *LASER: Creating Unity in Diversity*, National Catholic Conference for Interracial Justice (Washington, D.C., 1985). This is the story of a project created and implemented by a multicultural team that presents a format in which such exchanges can take place.

have spokespersons who can present their views and aspirations in ways that are easily understandable. Their religious experience and practices are often judged as faulty (based on superstitions) and immature, hence not having much to contribute to the faith community. To alter this perspective requires, then, that the first step be one of enabling the members of the mainstream Catholic groups to overcome stereotypes about racial and cultural minorities and to begin to accept them as equal members of the family of God, with gifts, rights, and responsibilities. At the same time, every effort has to be made to allow the ethnic groups to gain self-confidence and knowledge of what their gifts and contributions can be to this Church and culture.

This first step can be accomplished by engaging *all* groups in a catechesis of cultural literacy aimed at cultivating that respect of which the *National Catechetical Directory* speaks. All groups, not just those of the mainstream, are to participate in these efforts because it is a widely accepted fact among intercultural sociologists and anthropologists that every human group— regardless of how low or high on the economic or educational scale it may be—has perceived notions of which human cultures and races are worthy or unworthy of respect; which are valuable or useless; which are to be imitated or rejected. So, this first step is not to be seen as a requirement only of the mainstream culture, but of all cultural/racial groups. It is not to be assumed, for example, that Hispanics of different countries will be capable of relating harmoniously to each other just because they speak Spanish. We do not assume that Irish, English, Australians, Americans, and Indians will have instant affinity for each other because they speak English. Geography, history, and culture cause different nations of the same language family to be very different in religious outlook and practice.

To accomplish this first step, controlled communication and exchange of information between various groups are the most appropriate means. These exchanges must be designed specifically for the groups involved in a given community because the level of readiness for intercultural exchanges varies greatly from community to community. This readiness is shaped by the local history of the area, the nature of the reasons why certain ethnic groups have made their home there, and the openness and welcoming traditions of the host communities. All those factors must be carefully weighed and taken into account as steps are taken to create the atmosphere of mutual trust and respect between cultural groups that are basic to the development of a more catholic Church.

The second step is the continuously refined articulation of a vision of Church in the world that does not rest merely on the vision of the descendants of largely Northern European Catholics; but one that takes into account the faith, traditions, and talents of other Catholic groups from every corner of the globe that have made and are making their home here. The present vision of Church has been molded in an anti-Catholic environment shaped by the Protestant ethos and has, for the most part, tended to be private, apologetic, and defensive rather than social, assertive, and, at times, denunciatory. The recent pastorals on peace and the economy are indications that the Church in the United States is changing its perception of its role and is embarking on just such a journey of greater social responsibility and involvement.

One of the factors in this change could very well be the increasing number of bishops from minority groups in the ranks of the episcopacy. Another factor could be the increased contact between bishops of Latin and North America in the years following the 1968 Latin American Bishops' Conference at Medellin, which brought instant worldwide recognition to the role the Church can and must play in issues of justice and human rights. One could say that there has been already some progress toward intercultural dialogue and exchange of gifts at the level of the Church's hierarchy, and now the task is to achieve equal gains at the levels of the diocese, the parish, and educational establishments.

Biblical and Theological Foundations

The question of the need for multicultural catechesis is often asked, especially by those who have not had the opportunity to spend much time abroad nor had the benefit of experiencing firsthand the growth that takes place when one learns to see the world through different perspectives, or when one comes to understand the way in which God and the gospel message have been rooted in a different soil. For those who have come to know, understand, value, and respect what others have to offer, the question has been answered by the growth they have themselves experienced. They too, however, can learn from looking at the question from the perspective of the biblical and theological foundations of our Christian faith.

Our Christian view on life is grounded in the Bible, and in the theology inspired by the Bible as believers reflect on their following of Christ. The Christian perspective has been and continues to be shaped by the interplay of the different cultures. While the essential message of the Gospel is unchanging—what Pope Paul VI referred to as the "nucleus of the faith"—its richness cannot be fully comprehended or expressed by any one cultural form. The multicultural nature of the Church refers both to the catholicity of the Christian community and to the universal message of the Gospel.

The Christian mission is to make this catholicity a practical reality by ensuring that the Gospel is incarnated in all the cultures of the world—"Go into the whole world and proclaim the good news to all creation" (Mk 16:15). Failure to understand and accept the universal dimension of the message of salvation led to a severe identity crisis in the early apostolic community. It has been a serious stumbling block in the Church's missionary work. Here and now it challenges the attitudes of the mainstream cultures toward other expressions of the Gospel found among the many groups who form the Catholic Church in the United States.

The New Testament experience can help us reflect on the multicultural nature of the faith we profess. Luke tells us that Jesus was raised as a Jew according to the traditions of his ancestors. His language, thought patterns, and customs were Jewish. It was with this strong sense of Jewish identity that he began his mission. To his inner circle of disciples, Jesus disclosed that this mission was to preach the good news of salvation to his own people so that, through their acceptance, the nations would be led to faith.

This theme of the universality of the message of salvation disclosed by Jesus is the dominant theme of Luke's Gospel and of Acts. Luke describes the rejection of this message of universal salvation when Jesus preached in his own village in the synagogue of Nazareth in Galilee (Lk 4:14–30). The people rightfully understood Jesus' message as a challenge to their exclusive understanding of their relationship to God as expressed in their traditions. Jesus was stating that the "chosenness" of the Jewish people was not due to any innate superiority over other peoples but solely to their role in God's plan of salvation.

Although Jesus was accepted in faith and love by his inner circle of followers, they did not understand his inclusive approach to the nations (cultures) of the world. In the turning point of Mark's Gospel (ch. 8), Peter makes his profession of faith in Jesus as Messiah. But he rejects Jesus' interpretation of the Messiah as the suffering servant and earns a strong rebuke for trying to impose the common cultural understanding of what the role of the Messiah should be. Jesus understood very well how shocking the cultural implications of his message of universality were to his disciples. For this reason, he promised the gift of the Holy Spirit, who would give them understanding of his teaching and message. Although Pentecost was a transforming experience for the disciples, and even though they received the gift of tongues—a sign of universality—we know from Luke's account in Acts, they still did not understand the practical implications of the Gospel's universality. Luke dramatizes this lack of understanding in Acts 10:15 in what may be aptly seen as the identity crisis of the early Christian Church.

In the Cornelius event, both in Peter's vision and its aftermath at Cornelius' house, Peter was brought to realize that all God's creatures (cultures) were clean (good). The Cornelius event and Peter's defense of his actions in not fulfilling the prescriptions of the Mosaic law, joined to the preaching of the Gospel to the Gentiles and the establishment of a mixed community at Antioch, led to a crisis among the early Jewish Christians, which led to the calling of the first Council of Jerusalem. The decision of this council was not to require the cultural conversion of Gentiles as a condition for becoming Christians. This break from the cultural mold in which Christianity first took shape and the acknowledgment that Christian identity might have a plurality of cultural forms were decisive factors in the rapid spread of the faith. Many of the elements of our present liturgical celebrations were incorporated into the tradition as the Church moved, first through the Mediterranean world and later Northern Europe.

The basic theological principle underlying all multicultural catechesis gleaned from the New Testament is the incarnation itself. The recovery of this incarnational principle, through the reality of the multicultural presence of the Church's bishops at the Second Vatican Council, was the fundamental theological contribution of Vatican II.[3] The Council's *Decree on the Church's Missionary Activity* (*Ad Gentes*) best expresses this principle when it states that the Church "must implant itself among all [cultural] groups in the same way that by his incarnation Christ committed himself to the particular social and cultural circumstances of the people among whom he lived" (AG, 10). This insight was reiterated by Pope Paul VI on numerous occasions (i.e., "The Church is universal by mission and vocation . . . but she takes on different cultural expressions and appearances in each part of the world" [*Evangelii Nuntiandi*, 62]). And, in *Catechesi Tradendae*, Pope John Paul II has called us to look for those unique gifts that can only be found in other cultural perspectives: "Catechesis will seek to know these cultures . . . it will be able to offer these cultures the knowledge of the hidden mystery and help them bring forth from their own living traditions original expressions of Christian life, celebration, and thought" (CT, 53).

The image of a prism illustrates the value of the inclusion of all cultural groups in our catechesis. The gospel message is like a light refracted through the prism of humanity in all the changing colors of the cultures of the world and of our society. No one culture can fully express or contain the richness of the Gospel, but their different understandings complement one another to the enrichment of us all.[4]

This most dynamic and prosperous society of ours has been possible by the contributions and free interactions of ethnic groups. This interplay of cultures and ideas is constantly being celebrated through music, art, clothing, and food festivals, as well as through business, educational, and cultural exchanges on many fronts. Due to these free and varied intercultural interactions already happening in the secular realm, the Church in this country can become the laboratory within which the oneness of the human family can be modeled and effectively nurtured. The most important tool for the concrete realization of the gospel imperative to be

---

3. Karl Rahner, *Concern for the Church* (New York: Orbis Books, 1979), ch. 6, 7.

4. Austin Lindsay, "Biblical and Theological Foundations of Multicultural Religious Education," *Momentum* (February 1983).

one as the Father and Jesus are one (Jn 17:21) is a catechesis that has been designed with the potential as well as the hazards of the multicultural society in mind.

This is not an easy task, and one for which there are few ready-made answers. But, Jesus did not say that to follow him would be easy; he gave us, however, the total assurance of his presence as we go about the task of preaching the liberating Word that makes us all children of the same God: "Each of us here as divinely as any is here."[5]

---

5. Walt Whitman, "Of the Terrible Doubt of Appearances."

Native American Catechesis and the Ministry of the Word

Rev. Michael Galvan

The experience of God manifests itself both in individuals and in communities. For Roman Catholics, we experience God as individuals shaped by a common tradition and Scripture. However, each of us relates to tradition and Scripture in our own unique ways. Our faith, as a result, springs forth from a dialogue among the individual, the community, and God. In recent years, a greater sensitivity has appeared in regards to various cultures and languages. We have discovered that one's culture and language affect how one believes. In this article, I will explore how the culture of native Americans affects and contextualizes our faith.

In a person's faith life, we can discern various movements: initial conversion, times of rest, ever-deepening life-long conversion, and times of doubt and struggle. In every moment, however, we notice that humans respond to God's call. For Christians, the fullness of God's revelation is expressed in Jesus Christ.[1] Therefore, when we look at the New Testament, discipleship is characterized not by the memorization of certain principles or texts but by a life-long following and living with the Messiah. A Christian disciple is not bound primarily to a doctrine but to the person of Jesus. The call that Jesus issues to the disciples is a simple but profound one—"Follow me."[2] The question that faces Christians is, How do we follow Christ?

Jesus' directive was to continue the proclamation of God's revelation. To share in the mission of Jesus is to participate in proclaiming the Word,

---

1. Walter M. Abbott, SJ, ed., "Dogmatic Constitution on Divine Revelation" (*"Dei Verbum"*) in *The Documents of Vatican II* (Piscataway, N.J.: New Century Publishers, Inc., 1966), no. 2.

2. Xavier Leon-Dufour, ed., *Dictionary of Biblical Theology*, Second Edition, trans. by P. Joseph Cahill (New York: Seabury Press, 1977), p. 126.

in celebrating the sacred mysteries, and in serving one another. *Sharing the Light of Faith* points out three ministries that support these aspects of the Church's mission: the ministry of the Word, the ministry of worship, and the ministry of service.[3] While we distinguish these three ministries for the purpose of study and reflection, we need to remember that they are inseparably linked. We cannot proclaim the Word without putting the Word into concrete and particular actions. Furthermore, we cannot do either of these ministries without being nourished and challenged by a life of worship and prayer.[4]

As we can distinguish different movements in an individual's faith life, we can distinguish various movements in the ministry of the Word: pre-evangelization, evangelization, catechesis, reevangelization, and reconciliation. Catechesis presumes that individuals have already been converted to a faith in the Lord Jesus. What we encounter in catechesis is a deepening of an already existent faith. Catechesis speaks to the faith life of people and must, therefore, address the whole person: social, intellectual, emotional, spiritual, physical, and cultural. As Richard J. Hater writes, catechesis calls a Christian

> . . . to hear, understand, interiorize, and respond to God's word in acts of service and celebration. Catechesis simultaneously firms up individual faith and initiates into the community. If either of these is deficient, catechesis will not accomplish its full purpose.[5]

As a result, we need to address ourselves to the question of faith before we can determine the nature of catechesis. Especially since the Second Vatican Council, we have begun to move away from an understanding of faith as a belief in certain doctrinal statements to faith as a dynamic, living relationship with God. In the former understanding of faith, catechetics concerned itself with the transmission and memorization of data. Such an approach can be seen in such classic question-and-answer texts as *The Baltimore Catechism*. The catechetical language is definitional and has only one meaning. When faith is seen as relational, the element of mystery heightens; language becomes evocative and symbolic. *Sharing the Light of Faith: The National Catechetical Directory for Catholics of the United States* represents such an approach. When one takes into consideration native American traditions, the catechetical text *Builders of the New Earth*[6] be-

---

3. *Sharing the Light of Faith: National Catechetical Directory for Catholics of the United States* (Washington, D.C.: USCC Office of Publishing and Promotion Services, 1979), no. 30.

4. See my article, "Enculturating the Liturgy in North America," *Liturgy* (Washington, D.C.: The Liturgical Conference, 1986), pp. 41–45.

5. Robert J. Hater, *The Relationship between Evangelization and Catechesis* (Washington, D.C.: National Conference of Diocesan Directors of Religious Education, 1981), pp. 2–3.

6. John Hatcher and Patrick McCorkell, *Builders of the New Earth* (Rapid City, S.Dak.: Diocese of Rapid City, 1975).

16

comes not only possible but necessary. In this latter approach, catechetics calls forth transforming experiences.

This shift in catechetical approaches is discussed by Pope John Paul II in *Apostolic Exhortation on Catechetics*. While upholding the importance of the content of catechetical materials, Pope John Paul II maintains that adaptions may be necessary for the communication of the Gospel. Such adaptions may be necessitated by age, culture, language, or ecumenical concerns. In regards to cultural adaptions, he states:

> . . . catechesis will seek to know these cultures and their essential components; it will learn their most significant expressions; it will respect their particular values and riches. In this manner, it will be able to offer these cultures the knowledge of the hidden mystery and help them to bring forth from their own living tradition original expressions of Christian life, celebration and thought.[7]

If we follow the Holy Father's lead, it would not be an adequate proclamation of the Word if we were simply to utilize Western catechetical materials and not adapt them to the native American experience. If our goal is one of tranformation and not simply one of transmission, inculturation becomes a necessity.

This need to produce catechetical materials that would be developed primarily for native American peoples served as the motivating force behind a consultation with native American catechists that was held in November 1982. The Tekakwitha Conference served as the co-sponsor of the event along with the United States Catholic Conference's Department of Education. Sr. Mariella Frye, the USCC representative for Catechetical Ministry, reminded the native catechists that their work fit within the framework of the catechetical ministry of Jesus. As she stated:

> Like Jesus, the catechist begins with people's experience, sheds the light of the gospel message on that experience, and explains what Jesus is asking them to do when they follow him.[8]

The tension that has existed for native American Catholics has been well documented. One can read such classic works as *Black Elk Speaks*, *The Sacred Pipe*, and *The Sixth Grandfather* to see the Lakota holy man's

---

7. Pope John Paul II, "Apostolic Exhortation on Catechetics" in *Origins* 9:21, 329–348.

8. Sr. Mariella Frye, MHSH, "Native Catholic Catechesis: Tekakwitha Conference," *The Story and Faith Journey of Seventeen Native Catechists* (Great Falls, Mont.: Tekakwitha Conference, 1983), p. iv.

struggle.[9] Patrick Twohy's *Finding a Way Home*[10] illustrates this in a more contemporary setting. The experience of native peoples with the Tekakwitha Conference further substantiates this phenomenon. For many native American Catholics, the tension between practicing the native ways and the Catholic ways has been paramount. To deny either our native or Catholic roots causes some identity confusion. How does one be native and Catholic at the same time? How does one become transformed into Christ?

We need to remember that transformation, conversion, does not occur in relation to certain abstract principles but in response to one's experiences and stories. In other words, if native Americans are to be transformed, converted, to the Lord, this conversion must take place within the context of their own experiences and stories.[11] What types of experiences and stories do we need to address in a native catechesis?

First, we must realize that when we deal with native Americans, we are not encountering one culture. Each nation, tribe, and clan has its own particular and unique culture and tradition. The culture of the shepherding Navajo differs from the fishing culture of the Tlingit, and both differ from the hunting culture of the Lakota. It is important to attend to these tribal differences in catechetics. In addition, the degree of contact with the dominant Western culture varies. Some native Americans, especially those living in urban areas, may have lost, to some degree, contact with their roots. Yet, they experience some dissonance between their familial upbringing and the dominant culture.

Second, lest we lose all hope of successfully undertaking a native catechetical ministry, there are common threads and elements that native cultures share. We can distinguish the following common threads: the relationship with words (story), the relationship with time (expressed often in ritual), the relationship with the land, the relationship with all creatures. Let us discuss each of these elements in further detail.

My grandmother spoke in very few and short sentences. The multiplication of words destroyed the beauty and the sacredness of words. This reverence for the spoken word resulted from a deep reverence for breath. A person's breath expresses one's very life. So, words express one's very self, not merely one's thoughts and ideas. When these words create familial

---

9. John Neihardt, *Black Elk Speaks: Being the Life Story of a Holy Man of the Oglala Sioux* (Lincoln: University of Nebraska Press, 1979); Joseph Epes Brown, *The Sacred Pipe: Black Elk's Account of the Seven Rites of the Oglala Sioux* (New York: Penguin Books, 1971); Raymond DeMallie, ed., *The Sixth Grandfather: Black Elk's Teachings Given to John G. Neihardt* (Lincoln: University of Nebraska Press, 1984).

10. Patrick J. Twohy, *Finding a Way Home: Indian and Catholic Spiritual Paths of the Plateau Tribes* (Spokane, Wash.: University Press, 1983).

11. Cf. Donald Gelpi, *Charism and Sacrament* (Ramsey, N.J.: Paulist Press, 1976) and *Experiencing God* (Paulist, 1978); also, John Navone and Thomas Cooper, *Tellers of the Word* (New York: LeJacq Publishing, Inc., 1981).

and tribal stories, they express the very life of a people. As a result, native peoples tend to express themselves more in stories, in symbolic language. Such an approach is not counter to the Gospels but is rather similar to the manner of the New Testament. If we read the Gospels, we find Jesus constantly responding to people's questions with stories. The challenge of such an approach is that there can be many different interpretations of a story. As we mentioned above, though, such a symbolic approach characterizes present catechetical methods.

We cannot leave the relationship with stories at this theoretical level, however. For native peoples, not to tell our stories, not to live our lives out of our tribal stories, means that we experience a death to our full identity. We are both native and Roman Catholic. Catechesis, however, does not advocate the death of a culture. Instead, as Pope John Paul II has advocated, we need to utilize these stories to express the Gospel. I recall one woman religious asking me how this might be accomplished. A method I have found useful is to parallel the gospel stories to tribal stories. These stories enrich one another and empower a person to live by both stories: native and Christian.

In our immediate future, such a catechetical approach will present challenges. In a number of cases, textbooks, audiovisual materials, and other resources that express a native Catholic reality do not exist. So, we need to develop such materials. The Tekakwitha Conference serves as a resource in coordinating and producing the development of native materials. In the meantime, materials developed for the dominant Western culture may be used with some care and caution. With such a discerning use, the Western cultural expression of Christianity can be distinguished from the underlying realities of the Christian faith.[12]

Native traditions view time differently than the dominant Western tradition. While American society tends to view history as marching along in a linear fashion from point A to point E, native traditions view time primarily as cyclic. The chief question for native peoples is how to maintain the harmony and balance of creation as opposed to what am I suppose to accomplish. How we view salvation history is greatly affected by our view of time. For natives, the second coming is accessible at the present time and not only at the end of time. One does not simply look forward to heaven through the passage of time, but ones sees the beginnings of heaven here in a life lived harmoniously with all of creation.

The role of ritual is shaped deeply by such an understanding of time. Ritual does not set out to change reality but to maintain or reestablish the harmony of life. How do these rituals fit into Roman Catholic practice? I recall being present for a liturgy that utilized the blessing of water as its penitential rite. The blessing of water is seen as a purifying ritual,

---

12. Gilbert F. Hemauer, "A Cross-Cultural Approach to Catechesis among Native Americans," *The Living Light* 14:1 (Spring 1977): 136.

putting us back into harmony with creation. As we greeted the six directions, a certain centeredness was felt. Then, as we renewed our baptismal vows, I knew I was centered in creation and purified in the waters of baptism. Our task is to have our rituals reflect both our native and Catholic traditions.

Harmony with creation is grounded deeply in one's relationship with the land. For most native Americans, it is impossible to speak of a personal identity apart from the land. The earth grounds us not only geographically but also psychologically. As my grandmother told me, when I lost touch with Mother Earth, I misbehaved. When I attended to the land, however, my behavior improved. In other words, the land itself can heal.

While this phenomenon may be difficult for a nation comprised largely of immigrants, it cannot be minimized for native people. One is buried in the earth from which one was born. I was born from land nourished by my ancestors, and in my death and burial I will nourish the land for future generations. The land becomes the means for transcending time and reaching through to other generations. Such a sense of solidarity with former and future generations can only enhance our Christian faith in the Communion of Saints. Can we appreciate the land enough to be able to appreciate other Christian generations?

A caution must be issued here not to reduce this relationship with the land to mere romanticism. The land can be harsh and exacting as well as gentle and nourishing. Do we always see the land as our Mother? I recall being present at a meeting in Hoonah in the Juneau diocese. This wonderful woman stood up and spoke of the land and the very rocks as living beings. How can we move to such an understanding?

Finally, we need to address ourselves to our relationship with all of God's creation. Popular Western belief views humanity as the pinnacle of creation. If we were to draw this understanding, we would see a pyramid that illustrated the hierarchy of creation. If we were to draw a native American understanding of creation, we would see a circle. Humanity is not greater than or better than any other created being. Humanity shares the life of the Creator as do all creatures.

This past winter, I spent a week at the Kisemanito Centre in Grouard, Alberta, Canada. As I spoke of our native relationships with creatures, I could see an excited agreement appearing on the faces of the native participants. In Scripture, we find that Jesus utilizes such an approach: look at the clouds, see the mustard seed, observe the birds of the sky. Creation reveals God to us. For native peoples, one lives as part of the created order and not as ruler of it.

Thus, we find that a sound catechetical approach needs to be aware of the native relationship with story, ritual, land, and all created life. These relationships can affirm the gospel values and be deepened and transformed by the Gospel.

Third, a native American catechesis must challenge native peoples to examine our own traditions and cultures. As Jesus did thousands of years ago, the Gospel will challenge native peoples in the areas of justice, forgiveness, and healing. Any catechetical program must be willing to live out its prophetic role.

Fourth, the experience of native peoples takes place within the context of a tribe, clan, and family. Traditions are handed down from one generation to the next. As a result, an understanding of the Church as a community of believers handing on a faith in the Lord is greatly supported by native peoples. Can catechetics take advantage of such traditions?

Fifth, as I have argued that the dominant Western culture needs to become acquainted with native traditions, native peoples need to appreciate the beauty and giftedness of Western tradition. In dialogue with one another, each will grow and develop.

We can, thus, see that a native American catechetical method has various aspects. Catechesis needs to enflesh itself in the culture. A catechetical method must support communal life and the community's life of worship and prayer. Finally, a catechetical program must challenge native peoples to be of service to one another and to other cultures. When catechesis performs these functions, as native people, we will remember who and where we are and manifest the life of disciples of the Lord Jesus.

Cultural and Religious Practices of the Southeast Asian People

Rev. Umberto Nespolo, OMI

Jesus spoke in parables; it is the same way of the Asian people. Jesus presented all of his teaching in parable or story form, using symbols, similes, periphrases, and circumlocutions. The Asian people do not have concrete nominatives for intellectual experiences, ideas, or abstract nouns. That is why it is so very important to understand the many differences between the cultures of the East and West when working with the catechumen. This article is written with the hope that some of the flavor of the Asian language and imagery will be conveyed to the reader along with a catechetical message for those who work with and in the Asian Catholic community.

> O Lord, our Lord,
>> how glorious is your name over all the earth!
>> You have exalted your majesty above the heavens. . . .
>
> When I behold your heavens, the work of your fingers,
>> the moon and stars which you set in place—
> What is man that you should be mindful of him,
>> or the son of man that you should care for him?
>
> You have made him little less than the angels,
>> and crowned him with glory and honor.
>
> You have given him rule over the works of your hands,
>> putting all things under his feet:
>
> All sheep and oxen,
>> yes, and the beasts of the field,
> The birds of the air, the fishes of the sea,
>> and whatever swims the paths of the seas (Ps 8:2,4–9).

Little villages of Laos country with mountains that are covered with beautiful opium flowers. Little villages of Laos valley crossed by streams and rivers, sometimes lazy and quiet, sometimes torrential and whirlpooly with raging, running waters. Little villages on the great Mekong River, majestic and turbulent like an immense snake, always brown and full of many things taken from its banks throughout the many miles from China to the Vietnam Sea, where songs and sounds echo the endless stories of thousands of years—exciting stories and adventures of thousands of people who share with the great river the journey of their lives and their existences—to this, they entrust the daily experiences of hope and love, of life and death. Little villages of the Laos people (the French called it "country of the far north," but the real name is *Lang Sang:* "Kingdom of a Million Elephants"), always with a temple or pagoda in the center, where the gong (drum of the Buddhist monks), beaten with the strange and mysterious *tam-tam*, marks the principal hours of the day and night; warns and informs of the feasts, holidays, and religious celebrations; and makes sense and gives prestige to the turn of the seasons and to the events and history of the people.

Little Indochinese villages where one day the "Good News" arrives. The people, the houses, the temples, the streams and rivers, the fields and forests become adorned with new light and new warmth, and life becomes marvelous.

"Now I see; now I understand; now I'm full of joy; now we are living," declares Chang Zay, the old chief of the village of the "Moss Ox" mountain.

"Now we know why . . . now we know the meaning of our life on earth. Our traditions and our faith are now bright and confirmed . . . the same of our being. We wander and roam as man on earth, our conclusion and our destiny," proclaims the young man, Ong Chay, while we cross the forest to arrive in the village of Quiet Valley (*Nas Xang Ka*).

We pass a village where the people do not accept the message. All of the people—the old and the children—are sad, fearful, and timorous. Za Noua came to visit me one day. He wanted me to write a letter to the pope in Rome. "We are now believers, and so, we are now your children and children of the Church's family. . . . We are taking part in and cooperating in being builders of the presence of the Church of Jesus day after day with our living faith, our prayers, our offering, our suffering, and our practice of charity. Please, accept us, agree to our living work and bless us."

"Father," the people said to me, "now we need help to grow in our faith. For, we want to live the Christian life because now we know the truth and can see the good with God and Jesus as the light and the life. Before, we did not know because no one came to teach us—to live and to die was indifferent to us, in the same way as the animals. Please, do everything possible to help us, because we do not want to die; it is good for us to live in this new light."

I was reminded of the words of Isaiah: "The people who walked in darkness have seen a great light; upon those who dwelt in the land of gloom a light has shone. You have brought them abundant joy and great rejoicing" (Is 9:1-2).

One day, while we were walking through the forest from *Ban Houei Sek* (village of "blessing river") to *Nong Xang Ka* (village of "tranquillity"), Mr. Tong Xeng, a new convert, recited by heart the chapter of Tobit in which the Angel Raphael traveled with and accompanied Tobiah. Tong Xeng was a catechuman, and he will remain a catechuman forever because he was married to two women; he is a bigamist. He wishes to learn the catechism, and with a lot of effort, has learned to read a Bible translated into his language.

Za Noua, the shaman of *Kiuchatiam* (the "Moss Ox" mountain), was convinced by the fact that the Great Spirit, preached by the missionary, listened to his prayer for the return of good health to the missionary, who had become seriously ill. Za Noua had practiced the shamanism—rite for the spirits—for many hours, and the missionary recovered. This incident impressed the missionaries, who came to understand that the rite for the spirits is a prayer for the sick and the dying, with varied ceremonies that express the different attitudes and motivations of the prayers: praise, glory, petition, intercession, offering, and sacrifice. The rite to the spirits for those who are dying has two particular meanings: to accompany and give way to death to prevent getting lost in the forests or in the place of the bad "spirits"; to teach the spirit and soul about death so as to help it find the way back to the first forefather. For the Hmong people, this means to go back to the patriarch Abraham. This is why, for the Hmong people, we have two particular celebrations for death: the *Ka Ke Pa Tua*, the rite to help the soul through death, and *Ka Ke Xa Pli*, the rite to send an envoy of the spirit and soul back to the forefather, Abraham, in paradise, into the kingdom of God of eternal life. In these, and in many other circumstances of daily life of the Asian people, the Catholic faith has proven that much is complete and confirms evidence concerning human nature, in general and in particular.

In order to begin to understand the Asian people, one must recognize that much of the Oriental language is pictorial or symbolic rather than literal. By way of example:

- *Something beautiful* is depicted and represented by the flowers.
- *Something clear or bright* is represented by the light of the sun.
- *Serenity* is depicted by the nightly warmth of the moon.
- *Love* is represented by the red sunset; *goodness* and *bounty* by the breast and bosom of a mother.
- *Something mysterious* is represented by the twinkling of stars at night.
- *Thought* is depicted by the live eye; *word* by the noise and whisper of lovers or by the noise of spring rains.

- *Height* is represented by the summit of mountains.
- *Greatness* is represented by things such as the *Mykene* tree.
- *Hardness* is depicted by things such as the *Mydu*, hard wood into which it is impossible to rivet a nail, or by the hardness of a diamond.
- *Fear* and *fright* are represented by the trembling and rumbling of the thunder.
- *Hope* is represented by the tranquillity of the heart's certain waiting.
- *Heat* is depicted by the metal sending out sparks.
- *Fire* is represented by the forest or the field aflame and ablaze.
- *Life* is represented by the egg disclosing; *beginning* by the rising sun.
- *End* is depicted by the extremity of something.
- *Wish* and *desire* are represented by the rainbow or the snake with two heads.
- *Anxiety* is depicted by the rabid dog; *waiting* by the tiger lying in wait.
- *Woman* is represented by the spring or source; *man* by the fiery horse.

The missionary who announces the Good News needs to learn and understand the culture and customs of the people, to esteem and adapt, and to modify oneself to be able to present the reality of the Good News. As Paul wrote to the Corinthians: "I made myself the slave of all so as to win over as many as possible. I became like a Jew to the Jews in order to win the Jews. To those bound by the law I became like one who is bound (although, in fact, I am not bound by it), that I might win those bound by the law. . . . To the weak I became a weak person with a view to winning the weak. I have made myself all things to all men in order to save at least some of them" (1 Cor 9:19–20,22).

The missionary—well grounded and well founded in the words of Jesus and in the teaching of the Church; adorned with a unique symbol, the crucifix; bearing only one book, the Gospel—learns the language of the people, their culture and customs, their history, and their religion and traditions. And, in the same way as Jesus, he is then prepared to contact and meet the people, armed with a good comprehension and understanding of their ways, in order that he might gather and assemble every race and tribe to become disciples of Jesus and members of the Church within their own cultures and within their own riches.

The Asian Idea of God

The majority of the people of Laos belong to or are influenced by the Buddhist religion. One day, I saw that my students were upset and angry toward the foreigners. The Buddhist monks had told them that the Europeans had said that the Buddhist religion is atheistic. This is not true; the foreigners do not know the teaching of Buddha. The Veda *sutra/karma* teaching is "perfect existing and living is the Idea; the Idea of everything and every existence." Attracted by something material, a particle of the Idea becomes material in the universe. Attracted by something animal, a particle of the Idea becomes animal. Attracted by something human a particle of the Idea becomes human. Attracted by something extra, the particle of the Idea becomes mutable, changing from one state to another and starts into transmigration and reincarnation.

Buddha reached the conclusion: The attraction draws the particle of the Idea into becoming something material or animal or human and these material, animal, and human beings fall into trouble, pain, and suffering, then into transmigration and death because of the desire. With the Five Commandments, abstinence, and especially meditation, man will attain the "illumination." This means freedom, liberation, and redemption from all attractions and desires. Free from everything, man can go back and return into the perfect Idea, Nirvana, or paradise. This is not unlike Saint Thomas Aquinas' understanding of the "Idea" of God, Father Almighty, Creator of heaven and earth.

In 1972, Bishop Alessandro Staccioli, OMI, bishop of Luang Prabang, Laos, invited and accompanied some eminent Buddhist monks to visit the Vatican City and Rome. We were very surprised when they said, "Everything we see is great and beautiful, but nothing is interesting." We took them to visit the Benedictine monks in Cassino and the Franciscan friars in Assisi. After this, they declared, "You know, the most important experience was the meditation and contemplation. Now we see that the Catholic religion is very complete." For the Asiatic, the goal of a human being—man's beginning and his destiny, the dream of the human heart— is to become "Truth" through meditation and contemplation. The idea of both Jesus, the Saviour, and Buddha, the Illuminated: the human being wants to be delivered and redeemed.

Buddha is *not* a God. He is a man who discovered and envisioned a great way for liberation and redemption. Buddha did not write a book, but he transmitted his teaching to his disciples by preaching. The different statues and pictures of Buddha are representations and descriptions of Buddha's teachings. The statue of Buddha without arms, maimed of both arms, or with one hand up means detachment and separation—unworldliness and indifference to the attractions or desires of the human state. The Buddha seated means meditation, contemplation, and mystical practice. Buddha sleeping means illumination, peace and stillness, tranquillity and serenity. The meditation is not an effort to discover or to be thoughtful but is an extraction from and an indifference to oneself and everything else; purification and abstraction from everything material, animal, and human in order to be worthy to share the "illumination," to go back and reunite with the great Idea.

The relationship between the Asian religion and the Catholic faith is a mystical practice to discover God through and by Jesus in a personal way—a reality of human and Divine rapport; the relationship of a real

26

person to a real person (particle from and of the great Idea). It is the relationship to a real person who:

- knows you and you know him;
- understands you and you understand him;
- is interested in you and you are interested in him;
- contacts and speaks with you and you with him;
- trusts you and you trust him;
- believes in you and you believe in him;
- is committed to you and you are committed to him;
- plans a life program for and with you and you plan with him;
- takes care of you and you take care of him in a unique participation;
- unites or reunites with you and you with him;
- incorporates in you and you in him;
- is accomplished and realized in you and you are accomplished in and with him.

It is a relationship to a real person whose dimension is within you and your dimension is within him; whose joy is to stay with you and your joy is to stay with him in freedom, liberty, joy, and glory.

The rites of ablution and purification ordinarily are performed with perfumed water. For eight days, on the feast of the New Year, all of the people use and perform the rite of purification and renewal by blessing the statue of Buddha, the house, the temple, the public places, the schools, the offices, the soil, and the rivers. On the same occasion, all of the people go to the market and buy three or more little birds. They place their prayers and their confessions on the birds and, then, release the birds into the air. Or, the people go to the banks of the river and make heaps of sand. On the piles of sand they pray and make their confessions. When the first rain comes and the river overflows, the water will take away their prayers and confessions and the people will be purified.

At the beginning and the end of the Buddhist season of Lent (*Kao Pan Xa* and *Ock Pan Xa*)—the special time of purification and of special religious training in the Buddhist tradition—the people (in particular, the young people) prepare, with a great devotion, the bamboo sailboats covered with white paper. On the sides of the boat and on the mast, the people place, in order and in line, the white lighted candles. On the white paper, the people write their confessions, their promises, and their wishes. At nightfall, when the temple gong or drum signals the monks raising the prayer of *Sayanthro* or the prayer of blessing, the boats, all lighted, are sailed down the river. The people applaud, cry aloud, and pray. Slowly, the current of the river removes the lighted scene until it disappears, and the people go home joyful and satisfied.

Each day, during the season of Lent, *Kao Pan Xa*, early in the morning and again at sunset, the Buddhist monks preach and pray in *Phaly* (an old

Indian language used only for the basic Oriental language). Early in the morning, they walk in single file through the city or village to receive the offering from the people. This is the second great way or "vehicle" in the Oriental religion that allows the people a possibility of gaining a merit for the new and better life to come.

The Religious Feasts and Holidays

Like the feast days of the Catholic Church, the religious feasts in Asiatic countries are the most important traditions; they help to assemble the people into common-interest groups and qualify all religious, social, and political life.

Every temple or pagoda has a minimum of one particular feast for a period of from twelve to fifteen days. All of the people share and take part in the different ceremonies: blessings; visiting the temple (because every ornament and decoration, every sculpture and wood-carving are a *kerygma* and visible representation of the Buddhist doctrine); listening to the monks preaching; taking part in the different fun, play, and games; forming into a labyrinth to prove the personal destiny—the arriving in paradise or going into hell. The people dance the mythological and parareligious representations and tell stories and adventures. Ordinarily, they have a different kind of fireworks. Everywhere, there are stalls and booths for special foods, cakes, and every kind of drink. The parents bring their sons in front of the holy monk for a blessing and for dedication and consecration, especially at the time of puberty and adult age.

Other Special Rites

There are ceremonies to enter into the temple for prayers or for attending to the different needs of the temple; rites to request a visit to the monk (the monks never enter the homes of the people); rites for the proper reverence: kneel and crouch in the presence of the king, the monks, the authorities, and higher public and social superiors (for example, in the presence of the doctor); the joining of one's hands, as in prayer, at the forehead, at the mouth, or at the breast; rite of the meeting room or *sala*, to meet, listen, or ask for advice; rite of the father of the family to bless his house, his family, the field, and the sky for a new year or for a good crop; rite of the calendar with the different symbols of the years, especially at the birth of a white elephant—a sign of blessing and copiousness. There are other important rites and ceremonies: the large ceremony for the consecration of a young man to become a monk; the very interesting ceremony for the engagement and marriage; rite for death; rite for apprenticeship and anointment for a young man to become a member of the clan or tribe or to become a member of the council of the society; rite and ceremony for everlasting life—the *Daga*, a serpent and winding snake, comes from the *Pousy* temple into the royal temple of *Luang Prabana*, city of the king of Laos; special ceremony and celebration for the king of Laos, king and religious chief of the Buddhist Laotian people; the special rite and ceremonies for the angel *Theouada* at the particular temple in *Houei Say* city.

With the permission of our Holy Father, the pope, we have adapted many parts and aspects of the culture, customs, and traditions of the Southeast Asian people into the liturgical ceremonies and religious prepartions of the catechumens. In addition, the Asiatic influence is strongly evidenced in the construction of the churches.

Now, in many countries of the world, a great number of these people have become the poor refugees. "When we ran away and fled from our country because of the Communists," the people have said, "God protects us in the same way he protected the Israelites: 'The Lord preceded them, in the daytime by means of a column of cloud to show them the way, and at night by means of a column of fire to give them light. Thus, they could travel both day and night. Neither the column of cloud by day nor the column of fire by night ever left its place in front of the people' (Ex 13:21–22). When we were crossing the Thailand borders and frontiers, a thick fog closed in upon us to make us invisible to the Communists. For twelve long days we remained, day and night, hidden from the Communist soldiers, until we arrived and passed beyond the Thailand frontiers. We are six thousand persons, the complete families of many villages of North Laotian provinces. We will never forget this event and we will ever give thanks to God."

For the Southeast Asian peoples who are now refugees in the United States of America, the catechetical training and religious formation continues to grow, encompassing both the old traditions and evangelization.

II. LEADERSHIP DEVELOPMENT

Leadership Development in the Hispanic Community
María Luisa Gastón

Leadership for Liberation: Catechetical Ministry in the Black Catholic Community
Toinette M. Eugene, Ph.D.

Leadership and Professional Development in Light of the Native American Experience
Sr. Genevieve Cuny, OSF

Leadership Development in the Hispanic Community

María Luisa Gastón

To talk and write about leadership development in the Hispanic community is an exciting and yet risky enterprise. It is exciting because we are dealing with "living" tradition: the definite "textbook" theory has not been written yet; the pages are still being lived in the present-day experience of the Hispanic process. All of us, as pastoral agents, are part of this process as we plan our formation programs and our pastoral ministry, organize workshops, meet to analyze and evaluate our ongoing plans for leadership development. We often use an expression with our people: "We are making history . . ."

And, that is why it is also risky. At the local and national levels, history is still being written, various models of pastoral plans are being tested. Different approaches, based on analyses of needs, diverse cultural realities, and concrete objectives, are yet to be evaluated by the test of time and effectiveness.

I cannot presume, therefore, to give you a how-to formula that will encapsule this richness of the *Pueblo de Dios en Marcha* (People of God on the Move). Rather, what I am doing, as one who is part of that community and as a pastoral agent accompanying that process, is to share an experience. It is the experience of our pastoral team in the southeast region as we have tried to work with our people to empower them for ministry. We are a team made up of a priest, a sister, and four lay persons working together, witnessing to a model of Church of communion and participation, planning, discerning, praying, teaching, growing *with* our people and not just ministering *to* them, to enable and help them develop into active leaders, agents of their own communities.

Out of these experiences a frame of reference has emerged, a few "non-negotiable" principles, and several models that work for us and can be shared with others who hold the leadership development of the Hispanic community as one of their top priorities.

In this article, I hope to describe the elements of an effective leadership development for Hispanics, based on two main sources: (1) the historic process of the Hispanic Encuentros, especially the *III Encuentro* process and conclusions, and the Pastoral Plan being formulated at this time as a fruit of the *III Encuentro;* (2) the experience and models used by our regional team and the SEPI plan for pastoral ministry training.

Historical Context

Hispanics in the United States are in the midst of an ongoing grass-roots process of leadership development. The *III Encuentro Nacional Hispano de Pastoral* (Third National Hispanic Pastoral Encounter) is the most recent step in this history. Culminating in Washington, D.C. in August 1985 with the national meeting, the Encuentro included a three-year process of pastoral planning and team work at the grass-roots, diocesan, regional, and national levels. It prompted an outreach effort to the unchurched Hispanics and a period of study and reflection in small groups throughout the country, and led to diocesan and regional Encuentros. Finally, delegates from the more than 100 participating dioceses gathered at The Catholic University of America for a four-day experience of communal discernment, to arrive at the *National Pastoral Guidelines for Hispanic Ministry.*

One of the four objectives of the total Encuentro process was leadership development. The various steps of the process were planned and the methodology was chosen to promote this goal. It is a consistent thread running through the conclusions of the *I Encuentro* (1972) and the *II Encuentro* (1977). The process followed in the *III Encuentro* continued and improved upon that of the *II Encuentro*, which bore abundant fruits in mobilizing and training grass-roots Hispanic lay leaders throughout the country.

The *III Encuentro* Process: A Leadership Training Course

Did the Encuentro fulfill its goal of leadership development? Can the methods and models used be applied outside the context of the Encuentro to multiply the leadership development? The answers to both questions will be clear as we analyze various steps of the process.

1) The formation of a diocesan promoting team in each diocese to organize and coordinate the succeeding steps of the process in their diocese. These teams included lay persons, religious, and priests who were

already committed to the Hispanic ministry in the diocese, and who were already leaders in the various areas of pastoral ministry in the diocese. What is valuable from our perspective is that many of these people belonged to movements, parish and diocesan offices, and were probably doing "their own thing." The Encuentro brought them together to work as a team; to enlarge their vision and scope beyond their particular movement or ministry; to be trained and function in *pastoral de conjunto* (joint pastoral planning). The "EPD," as these teams were called, had to plan the various steps of outreach; analyze the reality of the diocese; organize the reflection groups and the diocesan meetings; train other small group facilitators; and compile the results of the surveys and meetings. They had to develop clear objectives, evaluate the process, and learn to work with each other to accomplish the task placed in their hands. In many dioceses, these EPDs have continued to function as diocesan teams after the Encentro and have elaborated and are implementing diocesan pastoral plans as fruits of the conclusions of their diocesan Encuentros. The obvious model to be learned from this is that of team ministry and *pastoral de conjunto* in which various areas of pastoral ministry (liturgy, catechesis, youth ministry, evangelization movements, social action, etc.) work together with a common vision and a united pastoral plan, ensuring the representation and participation of lay, religious, and clergy in the decision-making process as well as in the implementation of specific objectives.

2) The formation of mobile teams to reach out to unchurched Hispanics. Volunteers were trained as door-to-door evangelizers, going in teams of two to reach out to Hispanic families, sharing love and faith, and asking their participation in the process of the Encuentro by completing a questionnaire. Input from this questionnaire was then used to analyze the reality of Hispanics in the diocese and to choose priorities for further study. This model of grass-roots evangelization is very valuable for all of us concerned with the large number of Hispanics who do not participate in the life of the Church. The mobile teams taught us the important method of *going out* to the homes of Hispanics rather than waiting for them to come to us. Many parishes continue to use this evangelization team approach.

3) Many new leaders were trained in directing the small reflection groups to study the Encuentro themes. In regional and diocesan workshops, they learned how to facilitate the process of *Ver, Juzgar, Actuar* (See, Judge, Act); that is, to first look at and analyze their concrete reality; then discern and make a judgment on it in the light of faith, gospel values, and church documents; and, lastly, make a decision for action, spelled out as concrete pastoral commitments.

The Encuentro themes studied in these small groups included the areas of evangelization, social justice, youth, integral education, and formation of leaders. The materials, outlined at a national meeting from the grassroots consultations, were edited by our southeast regional team and prepared both on the popular level and in manuals for the use of the small-group leaders. Both the process of analysis/reflection/action and the study materials are valuable beyond the context of the Encuentro and can serve as excellent tools for leadership training of Hispanics.

It is worthy noting here that the leaders were trained not to make the decisions themselves but to *facilitate* the process so the people would do it; thus, the prophetic voice would emerge from the grass roots.

Another important element here is the change from massive church groups with passive participation to smaller groups and communities that foster the active participation of all, in which each person is valued, respected, and urged to engage in critical reflection and communal commitment for action. Out of these reflection groups, true Christian communities have been formed, continuing the process of evangelization and conversion.

I cannot stress enough that leadership development should aim at the formation of leaders for the building and nurturing of these small ecclesial communities. This has been a priority in the Hispanic pastoral process since the *II Encuentro*. We are also seeing this thrust toward small Christian communities, which originated in Latin America, spreading throughout the universal Church. Pope Paul VI, in *Evangelii Nuntiandi,* recognized the ministry of "leaders of small communities" as one of the new ministries that are most precious for the life and growth of the Church in our times. (EN, 73).

4) Training group facilitators for the diocesan, regional, and national Encuentros. In order to ensure the model of communion and participation in the various Encuentros, leaders were trained in communication skills, in communal discernment, in helping groups reach decisions by consensus, in summarizing and unifying conclusions, etc. They were trained to co-ordinate the process from small subgroups of 15 persons, to groups of 50, to miniplenaries of 200, to large plenary sessions of up to 1,000 persons. All of these groups were led by grass-roots facilitators, previously trained in special workshops with the use of guidebooks prepared by the national facilitating team. These, mostly lay Hispanics, emerged from within the Encuentro process itself and were empowered by it to continue as leaders in their own local communities after the Encuentro.

As a member of the national facilitating team, I saw this process taking shape and participated actively in designing it. We saw clearly that leaders are not born, they are made by doing. By training them and giving them the responsibility of carrying out the task at hand, motivated by faith and a deep love for their brothers and sisters, these Hispanic men and women—youth and adults of various nationalities, with or without much formal education, from rural and urban communities—could effectively serve as leaders and be forever transformed in so doing it.

This kind of process, which guarantees that all the participants are able to contribute their insights and ideas in an atmosphere of equality and collaboration, is truly a method coherent with the message of a Church of communion and participation and, as such, can serve as a model for leadership development beyond the Encuentro process.

From this brief and incomplete analysis of the *III Encuentro* process, one can nevertheless conclude that it did fulfill its goal of fostering the leadership development of Hispanics. The various training manuals, guidebooks, study materials, in addition to a wealth of other materials prepared by the regional offices and the national teams, can serve as models for the ongoing formation and development of new leaders.

The Regional Experiences of Leadership Development

Leaving the larger picture of the Encuentro process, let us now zero in on the experience of our regional pastoral team and of the Southeast Pastoral Institute.

Although in other regions of the country the ministry to Hispanics has a much longer history, our regional office and institute are the fruits of the *II Encuentro Nacional* in 1977. There were three dioceses with some Hispanic ministry at that time. At present, twenty-four of the twenty-five dioceses in the southeast region have some form of Hispanic pastoral activity, with different dioceses at varying stages of organization. With the impetus and the vision of the *II Encuentro* fresh in their minds and hearts, the regional team started to organize and develop the Hispanic leadership in each diocese. It is often easier to start from ground zero than to try to change and renew old structures and methods of ministry. So the Southeast has always had that advantage: to be able to start new, putting our own creativity, our own principles and methods to work in the leadership development of Hispanics in most of our dioceses.

What are some of the effective principles and models of leadership development that we have implemented in our region?

1. Diocesan Hispanic Pastoral Councils

Most of the dioceses of the Southeast are in the "Baptist Belt," with only about 3% to 10% of the population being Catholic. In many of these, there are few or no clergy or religious who speak Spanish and are trained for Hispanic ministry. Our people's resource, then, has been interested lay persons eager to help and to serve in ministering to their Hispanic brothers and sisters. This has been a blessing, promoting shared-team ministry rather than assigning the organizational task to *one* diocesan director.

The first priority when organizing Hispanic ministry has been to form a diocesan Hispanic council or committee of interested persons to help in the planning and implementation. The objectives given to this group are to analyze the reality of the Hispanics in the diocese; to identify and prioritize their needs; to organize themselves in teams or working groups to begin some concrete pastoral activities, especially the task of reaching out to unchurched Hispanics.

Our team maintained close contact through periodic visits, providing training for planning and motivation based on a common vision of the mission of the Church, and ongoing evaluation. The leadership and pastoral ministry were developed in the following areas:

- Spanish liturgies with a variety of liturgical ministries.
- Small groups and communities for prayer, study, and support.
- Catechesis for children and adults, including sacramental preparation, all in Spanish.
- Social/cultural events in which the cultural traditions and feasts are celebrated. These also serve as gathering points for families not yet involved in the ministry and as new contacts with unchurched Hispanics.
- Ministry to the needy, which they have identified in their original analysis of reality. We stress very strongly that the community should identify those Hispanic groups that are the most marginalized in their community to plan appropriate service to them. For some dioceses, these are refugees or new immigrant families or undocumented aliens. In other dioceses, this takes them to hospital ministry or prison ministry or ministry to handicapped children or migrant farm workers.

All of these pastoral activities are planned and coordinated through the representation in the Hispanic Pastoral Council, fostering cooperation, unity, and the use of various gifts and talents.

To summarize, then, the experience of organizing Hispanic ministry in the dioceses of the Southeast has led us to choose the following elements of leadership development as essential:

- Analyze reality as the foundation for actions.
- Provide doctrinal formation that stresses the communitarian model of Church; the evangelizing mission of all Christians; growth in spirituality of the leaders and the community; commitment to justice and service.
- Begin to work together in some chosen pastoral activities that will provide common goals and promote the emergence of new leaders.
- Organize around a diocesan council or team to integrate the various ministries in a common vision, as well as provide ongoing planning and evaluation in a *pastoral de conjunto*.

It is out of these experiences in ministry and service that further needs for formation and training emerge, such as leadership training in specific ministries of liturgy, catechesis, etc. Eventually, the diocese will have sufficient leaders and pastoral personnel to be able to set up a school of ministry (explained later on).

2. Youth Leadership Development

Youth ministry, though it could be included above as one of the many possible areas of ministry, deserves a separate section because of the numbers involved and because of the role it can play in the effective pastoral ministry to Hispanics. More than 50% of the Hispanic population in the United States is under the age of twenty-five. Therefore, youth ministry has been one of our top priorities. A specific approach is needed because of the unique problems of cultural identity, family relations, and societal pressures that Hispanic youth face in our times.

Our regional team, through its mobile team of youth ministry, has developed several models for the development of youth leadership.

Día de la Amistad (Friendship Day). A one-day retreat/workshop to convoke, motivate, and begin the process of youth-group formation in a diocese.

Experiencia Cristo. A weekend "Christ Experience" combining personal reflection, group dynamics, and key talks to deepen the process of conversion and commitment to youth ministry in a diocese. The weekend is planned and the talks given by a team of youth ministers who have undergone previously the experience and have been trained to conduct it, with the guidance of the regional team. In some dioceses, more experienced leaders have organized mobile groups to travel to neighboring dioceses for the *Experiencia Cristo,* as a missionary service.

Pascua Juvenil. A seven-week program of group reflection, prayer, and commitment for use during the seven weeks of Lent. Each year the *Pascua* tries to discover and deepen a different aspect of the Paschal Mystery. The themes and activities are developed by youth groups from participating dioceses, then the regional office unifies and publishes it. A whole process of leadership development is inherent to this program as the youth groups learn by doing, and then the regional team gives workshops to leaders to train them in the use of the materials. The *Pascua* process has three objectives: (1) to strenghten and renew the enthusiasm of already established youth groups as they receive formation in the central themes of Christianity; (2) to atract youth who do not belong to any group; (3) to form new groups with the leadership of some of the young people who already belong to other groups and who have participated in the *Pascua* in previous years. SEPI has published six *Pascuas.* Many dioceses throughout the country find the material quite useful for their youth ministry, and I myself have used it with a small adult Christian community with equally fruitful results—with some minor adjustments.

Annual Regional Youth Encuentro. A weekend limited to leaders of youth groups, for exchange of ideas, evaluation, and future planning, in addition to being an opportunity for further formation and leadership training.

Hispanic Youth Ministry Course. A one-week intensive course for youth leadership training offered every year by SEPI, which includes two days of Ignatian retreat. Other shorter workshops are offered when requested.

Hispanic Youth Ministry for Adult Advisors. We have found that specific training is needed for adult advisors of youth groups to renew their vision of Church, their pastoral principles, and their methodology and, thus, train them to facilitate and assist the life of the youth groups.

We have found that in some dioceses the vitality and commitment of the youth who are well organized provide the motivation to adults for a flowering of ministries in the dioceses, as well as being at the forefront of the organization and integration of the diocesan council. We have also found that the youth leaders of the past become the adult leaders of today, with tremendous leadership experience and with an up-to-date vision of Church.

3. Schools of Ministry

As the Hispanic ministry in a diocese develops, organization grows, and ministries multiply, the pastoral ministers and the communities detect the growing need for a more formal program of formation and specific training in various areas, leading to a certification and commission to serve as lay ministers in response to the needs of the diocese. Such a program is what we in the southeast region and in other regions of the country call the *Escuelas de Ministerios*. The U.S. bishops, in their pastoral letter, *The Hispanic Presence: Challenge and Commitment*, explain very clearly that the essential goal of the schools is to promote talented and committed individuals as leaders at the service of their communities" (pp.16-17).

Prior to the *III Encuentro*, only three dioceses in the Southeast had organized schools of ministry, with the assistance of the regional office. Sparked by the *III Encuentro* process and the commitment to promote leadership training, three other dioceses have now organized the schools of ministry, under the direction of and with the professors provided by SEPI.

Although each diocesan program is slightly different in length, requirements, and scheduling, they are guided by the same basic objectives as our Pastoral Institute:

● Provide a core doctrinal content on the Bible, Christology, ecclesiology, and pastoral principles;

- Provide leadership skills in communication, group process, pastoral planning, team work;
- Train participants to analyze critically their cultural values and traditions and their local reality to provide more effective and integral evangelization;
- Emphasize the experiential dimension of spiritual growth, personal ongoing conversion, commitment to community building, and a serious commitment to service;
- Provide specific training in a variety of ministries such as catechesis, youth ministry, liturgical ministries, small-community leaders, according to the talents of the person and the ministries needed in the community.

The schools of ministry are proving to be an effective model of formation for action, generating both enthusiasm and commitment in their participants.

4. SEPI: The Southeast Pastoral Institute

SEPI was born in 1979 as an answer to the needs of the Hispanic population of the southeast region and as fulfillment of the recommendations of the *II Encuentro*. As the *SEPI Catalog* expresses it, our first objective is "the development and renewal of Hispanic leadership for the integral evangelization of the Hispanic people." One of its priorities is to "recognize, promote, and encourage the local leadership throughout the region" (*SEPI Catalog*, p. 39).

How does SEPI accomplish this leadership formation? In determining the objectives and programs of the Institute, the pastoral team wanted to encompass the following three dimensions for a truly integral leadership formation.

The Experiential Dimension. SEPI tries to facilitate an experience of faith and community. We try to create an atmosphere of Christian community among the faculty, staff, and participants, through prayer, faith sharing, interpersonal dialogue, retreats, and other activities. We aim at the deepening in faith of the pastoral agents, so that their option for Christ will be reinforced and their commitment to be part of the pastoral ministry of the Church for Hispanics will be renewed.

The Academic Dimension. The academic program is composed of core courses, electives, and skills workshops, which the student may take in accordance with the program level. There are three possible programs:

a) Master of Arts in Pastoral Ministry for Hispanics, accredited through Barry University in Miami. We want to provide the opportunity for qualified Hispanics who have completed a bachelor's degree to obtain this advanced academic degree. In 1983, SEPI became the first institution in the nation to graduate students with this specialization, totally in Spanish, with the best Hispanic professors, specialists from throughout the world in their field of study, and at a very moderate cost. SEPI masters graduates are leaders in various pastoral ministries, directors of religious education, teachers in Catholic schools, leaders of movements and of small communities, and parish pastoral ministers. Some are businessmen and professional women who are making a Christian impact on society.

b) Certificate in Pastoral Ministry for Hispanics. There are many Hispanic leaders who only completed high school. Although the undergraduate credits do not lead to a bachelor's degree, the program prepares them to be even more qualified and effective ministers in a variety of pastoral activities.

c) Audit noncredit level. While we offer the advanced degree and certificate, we also want to reach the popular level participants: students not interested in or able to receive credits, but desirous of renewing their vision of the Church and becoming pastoral agents in the service of their communities. During the year, we provide shorter noncredit courses on topics of present interest in the Church and in Hispanic ministry, as well as those requested by the students in the evaluations after each course.

The Pastoral Dimension. It is the application through action of the academic study and the lived experience. It is a combination of doctrinal principles, strategies, methodology, skills training, and concrete action. We use an active methodology in our courses so that not only the content but the method itself is a source of leadership training for the pastoral minister. All the participants are challenged in the courses and in their research to bring out the pastoral implications for their specific ministries. Even those who say they come for personal enrichment and are "non-committed" are urged to make a ministerial commitment. Our aim is to offer a formation that leads to action, not just to increased knowledge.

These three dimensions of the SEPI program are not separate but rather are interrelated and evident in each of the courses and other SEPI activities. Thus, they fulfill the SEPI objectives already summarized when discussing the schools of ministry.

5. SEPI Video Ministry and Publications

Another instrument for the leadership development of Hispanics is the video production and the SEPI publications. We have produced more than sixty videotapes with the same professors who teach the courses on topics such as the Bible, spirituality, social doctrine, catechesis, the Sacraments, and others. They have been used in the schools of ministry and for group reflection and study in dioceses throughout the country. The *Pascua Juvenil* and other publications for adult evangelization and small-group discussion are also needed instruments for leadership training of Hispanics.

Conclusions: Elements of an Effective Leadership Development

From our regional experience and from the *III Encuentro* process, what are the essential elements for an effective development of Hispanic leaders? It seems to me, in summary, that there are six essential goals to strive for:

1) Recognize and foster the diversity of gifts among Hispanic leaders, empowering them for service in a variety of ministries in Church and society, so they may be able to use "the special gifts that Hispanics bring to the Body of Christ" (*The Hispanic Presence*, p. 3).

2) Promote leaders from the grass roots, from their local community, who know and live the culture and reality of that community and who are trained to plan their pastoral ministry based on an in-depth analysis of that reality.

3) Provide a doctrinal frame of reference for our leaders through biblical, theological, and pastoral formation, leading to a solid vision of the mission of the Church with emphasis on: the evangelizing missionary activity; formation of small ecclesial communities; commitment to justice for the transformation of society; commitment to service of the poor and marginated.

4) The process and methodology of pastoral ministry has to be coherent with the content of the message. The leaders need to be trained in human relations, communications, group participation, and team ministry, so that the way in which they serve gives witness to the model of Church of communion and participation.

5) The *Mística* in our ministry became even clearer after the Encuentro, during the process of theological-pastoral reflection. The leadership training of Hispanics must include and emphasize the spiritual growth, the personal and communal conversion which gives "soul" to the knowlege and pastoral actions.

6) *Pastoral de conjunto*, the phrase without translation, has been one of the fundamental fruits of the Hispanic process. Leaders must be aware of and committed to the total pastoral process of the Hispanic people, concretized at this time in the national Pastoral Plan and the diocesan plans. This unified pastoral planning is implemented through the formation of pastoral councils at the diocesan level, with representation and participation of all areas of ministry toward a common goal.

These are the "what" of leadershp development; How about the "who"? Who are the people we are trying to reach, to develop as leaders? The *III Encuentro Guidelines* spell out the priority groups: families, youth, women, and the poor. These are not to be just the recipients of our ministry, but the *agents* of ministry among Hispanics. Those responsible for planning the formation programs need to ask: Who are the poor, the marginalized, those not being ministered to in your specific area of the country or local community? In organizing our leadership programs and selecting the candidates, we need to make a consious effort to seek out and include potential leaders from these priority groups so that they may be trained and commisioned, empowered, to serve effectively the needs of these marginalized groups and guarantee their participation in the decision-making and pastoral-planning processes of the diocese.

Of the various models of ministry presented, the team ministry model seems to respond better to this urgent need for leadership development of the marginalized groups. At this moment of our church history, too many are excluded from the "official" authority for decision making in ministry, either because they are poor or uneducated or because they are women.

By forming teams and training our leaders to work in teams in our parishes, dioceses, and regions, in whatever pastoral work we do, we can ensure that the poor, the marginalized, the women, the youth, and people of various races and educational levels are included in the discerning and decision-making process for ministry; thus, all are enabled to share their gifts and charisms for the building of the kingdom and the transformation of society.

Leadership for Liberation: Catechetical Ministry in the Black Catholic Community

Toinette M. Eugene, Ph.D.

Every experience of positive leadership in the black community since its involuntary importation to this country in 1619 has been inevitably linked to an expression of liberation and to a theology of hope. "Follow the North Star" was the invariable directive offered by abolitionist Harriet Tubman in leading hundreds of black families to freedom on the Underground Railroad prior to the Civil War. "I leave you love," was the indisputable legacy left by educator Mary McLeod Bethune to thousands of black college students whose careers had been immeasurably limited by segregated schooling until the second half of this century. "We Shall Overcome" was the signature song of countless black preachers, teachers, and civic leaders who supported the Civil Rights movement of the 1960s, which ultimately has affected the destinies of all who have experienced any form of oppression and marginalization in this land that has historically proclaimed "liberty and justice for all."

These epigrams are but a few innumerable examples of leadership for liberation within the context of the black community in the United States. In a very broad sense, these examples also may be understood as a basis for the ministries of education and evangelization exercised by leaders within the black churches.

Similarly, patterns of professional, prophetic leadership have continually emerged from the midst of the American black Catholic community. Despite racist restrictions from both Church and society, witnesses of hope and testimonies of truth aimed at educating and evangelizing both the oppressed and the oppressor are abundant in the accounts of courageous foundations of religious orders for black women and the extraordinary priestly ordinations of black men in the nineteenth century. The early leadership of Fr. Augustus Tolton, Sr. Elizabeth Lange, and Sr. Henriette Delille, to name a few, attests to the leadership response of black Catholic people desiring to serve the Church.

The formation of five Black Catholic Lay Congresses, begun in 1889 under the direction of Daniel Rudd, took initiative in pointing out educational concerns and evangelization needs of the black community to the American hierarchy. These gatherings set an organizational example for the development of leadership for liberation in the diverse national organizations of black Catholics today.

The distinctive membership and purposes of the Knights and Ladies of St. Peter Claver, the National Black Sisters' Conference, the National Black Catholic Clergy Caucus, the National Office for Black Catholics, the National Black Lay Catholic Caucus, the National Black Catholic Seminarians' Association, and the National Black Catholic Administrators' Association represent the broadest spectrum of contemporary black Catholic leadership engaged in the liberating ministries of education and evangelization. It is precisely this collective body of persons that is primarily referred to by black Catholic bishops in their recent pastoral letter on evangelization, *What We Have Seen and Heard*. In describing the great need for and difficulties of promoting gifted indigenous leadership working with the black community in order to catechize and evangelize well, the bishops note:

> Since African-American members of the American Church are to assume the responsibility to which the Church and our racial heritage call us, black leaders in the Church—clergy, religious and lay— need encouragement and the authorization to use their competencies and to develop their expertise. Unhappily, we must acknowledge that the major hindrance to the full development of black leadership within the Church is still the fact of racism.[1]

Through a reassessment of meanings surrounding our understanding of indigenous catechetical leadership for liberation, and by a revision of religious experience, I shall offer some guidelines in this essay for developing a plan of action intended to support and enhance more effective black Catholic catechetical leadership.

1. A Reassessment of Meanings

Indigenization and Black Catholicism

The term *indigenization*, as used in its fuller sociological sense, indicates and characterizes a product or a socialization process that is "native-born."

---

1. *What We Have Seen and Heard: A Pastoral Letter on Evangelization from the Black Bishops of the United States* (Cincinnati: St. Anthony Messenger Press, 1984), p. 19.

It must be produced naturally in the environment in which it is found. Indigenization implies a people with a culture developed by themselves and enriched by their own past history and by the roots of their own religious traditions. In reexamining indigenization and its relationship to an authentic black articulation of the Christian faith, liberation theologian J. Deotis Roberts comments:

> Indigenization is a key concept for black theology [and catechesis] as it is for all socially conscious programs in theology. There have been several attempts to indigenize theology in recent years. This process is essential whenever theology becomes more than an exercise that is rational and abstract. . . . What we have in mind when we refer to "indigenization" is more ambitious and conscious. It is a deliberate acceptance of "context" or "situation" as the matrix of theological discourse.[2]

Some black Catholic bishops have written and spoken extensively on the problems due to the lack of indigenous process and the need for its implementation within the Catholic Church in order to strengthen evangelization and catechetical, pastoral leadership within the black community. Bishop James P. Lyke, OFM, has stated:

> If dignity and humanity are to be affirmed in any kind of consistent and coherent way, the indigenization of the Church must take place at every level. . . . That which is of universal character within the Church must be expressed in the language, form, and culture of the people. St. Augustine said, "God speaks to his people in the way people speak to themselves."

> We face no greater handicap . . . than the failure of the American Church to undertake seriously the process of indigenization, of power and decision-making authority, of the clergy and leadership in general, of liturgy, of education, of catechesis, and of service.[3]

An articulation by black Catholic people educating each other and the larger Church about God, interpreting freely and creatively the Word of God with approval and approbation from the institutional Church, is the intent of an indigenous catechesis.

---

2. J. Deotis Roberts, *A Black Political Theology* (Philadelphia: Westminster Press, 1974), p. 29.

3. James P. Lyke, OFM, "Application of Black Cultural Considerations to Catholic Worship" in *This Far by Faith* (Washington, D.C.: National Office for Black Catholics/The Liturgial Conference, 1977), p. 56.

Catechesis and Black Evangelization

The National Office for Black Catholics has previously published an excellent monograph entitled *Black Perspectives on Evangelization of the Modern World*, which may now be viewed as an appropriate companion piece for the black pastoral letter, *What We Have Seen and Heard*. By very adroitly offering an emphasis on the relational aspects of evangelization, it serves to further elucidate the black bishops' message as central to the religious well-being of the black community. The NOBC document explains:

> Evangelization . . . involves the continuing formation of the Christian community to a conformity with Christ and the principles of the Gospel, in an attempt to bring men [and women] into new relationship with one another through their common commitment. This community constantly extends itself, witnessing to the establishment of a new covenant—a reconstructed order in which every man [and woman] is free to live out the fulness of God-given dignity.[4]

In focusing on the establishment of a liberated community and on a reconstructed external social order, the NOBC also lays a parallel understanding to the *Sharing the Light of Faith: National Catechetical Directory for Catholics of the United States*, which links catechesis with evangelization, although by emphasizing primarily internal ways. *Sharing The Light of Faith* states:

> Although evangelization and catechesis are distinct forms of the ministry of the Word, they are closely linked in practice. Evangelization . . . seeks to transform humanity from within . . . it aims at interior change, conversion of the personal and collective conscience of the people . . . and the lives and concrete milieux which are theirs.[5]

The clarity and insistence of the NOBC document, which links evangelization and catechesis to prophetic action on behalf of justice, are significant. Catechesis and evangelization as distinct and yet related forms of the ministry of the Word require an acknowledgement that we are serving and encouraging a people who find and need political, economic,

---

4. *Black Perspectives on Evangelization of the Modern World* (Washington, D.C.: National Office for Black Catholics, 1974), pp. 6-7.

5. *Sharing the Light of Faith: National Catechetical Directory for Catholics of the United States* (Washington, D.C.: USCC Office of Publishing and Promotion Services, 1979), no. 35. This statement of the American Catholic bishops is based on *The General Catechetical Directory*, approved by Pope Paul VI, and also reflects the deliberations and conclusions of the 1977 International Synod of Bishops on "Catechesis in Our Time."

and social power as indispensable for the expression of our obedience to the Word of God.[6]

2. A Revision of Experience

Catechesis is "a form of the ministry of the Word that proclaims and teaches . . . leads to and flows from the ministry of worship . . . and supports the ministry of service,"[7] according to the definition of *Sharing the Light of Faith*. In planning for an indigenous catechesis that can serve effectively to lead a people toward liberation of all that is oppressive in their life experience, it is necessary to establish a firm basis that is at once black as well as Catholic in the universal sense. Such a liberating catechesis must be steeped in the experiential knowledge of the word of Scripture, which has been the strength and consolation of black people since slavery.

The point is that such a catechesis must of necessity give us a new way of looking at God's revelation through our blackness. And, what issues from this liberating perspective and leadership must be rooted and grounded not in black nationalism and ethnocentrism but in the incarnation, life, death, and resurrection of Jesus Christ and shaped to the realities of black life and thought. Consequently, effective catechetical leadership for liberation in the black community must be able to tell the sacred story of God convincingly and to connect it clearly with the story of black folk.

The story of divinity discloses not only that God has a predilection for the poor and the oppressed but also that God chose to become one of us. The sacred story reveals that God, in Christ Jesus, chose to suffer and die for us so that our people could be proud of our own humble condition, of our humiliation endured, and of our own hope for resurrection and liberation that is rooted deep within us. Because of this salvation history, which is recalled and handed on through an indigenous leadership within the black Church, we are able to respond, "We are Somebodies!" Because this sacred story has affected irrevocably the story of our black folk, we are able to say with feeling, "I may be poor, I may be struggling, but it won't matter. Somebody told me I'm a Child of the Most High. Somebody told me I'm lookin' good—made in the image of God!"

It follows that the understanding of God's self-revelation and of the redemptive mission of Jesus only can occur fully in a context in which black people can perceive God's presence and action in our lives. The knowledge of God and of Jesus Christ, after hearing this Word proclaimed

---

6. Gayraud S. Wilmore, "Three Considerations for a Black Christian Education Program." Talk delivered to Consultants for Black Christian Education (sponsored by JED, CE:SA) held at Scarritt College in Nashville, Tennessee, October 2, 1982 (photocopy), p. 2.

7. *Sharing the Light of Faith*, no. 32.

and handed on through indigenous catechetical leaders, is verified primarily by the circumstances in which black people's lives are lived. Perhaps, an authentic catechetical leadership has been so difficult to maintain and to bring to maturity in the black Catholic community not because black people have rejected the teachings of the Church but because the symbols of our faith, the stories of Scripture, and the sacramental rituals of the Church have only recently begun to be celebrated creatively or interpreted properly from the perspective of black experience and cultural patterns.

Through making explicit linkages and effective connections between black life-stories and the story of God's expressed affection for a Chosen People, we will be more enabled to reverence and communicate faith in a language that is sensitive to and significant for black people. By reechoing or handing on this sacred Word in this indigenous fashion, catechetical leaders in the black community will offer more effectively an approach to growth in faith as well as education for liberation.[8]

3. A Refining of Purpose

In presenting a refinement of purpose for developing indigenous leadership in the black Catholic community, and in raising the question of what must be developed as a further educational praxis, it is important to restate concisely some essential elements necessary for an effective black catechesis.[9]

There is a need for stressing the primacy of the black experience. The black experience is a source for training religious leaders and catechists because it seeks, when properly and fully developed, to relate the situation of black people in America to the biblical Word and to ongoing revelation. This means that a black Catholic catechesis cannot speak of the words and deeds of God without identifying this with the liberation of the black community and of all oppressed communities. The knowledge of black history, religious and secular, is essential for those who lead and teach in the black Catholic community. It is necessary because it displays clearly the determination of a people who would be liberated from all oppression.

The development of black culture is an essential element to be expressed within the context of a black catechesis. Culture, which shapes the ethos of a people, simultaneously forms and reflects its values. It also determines a people's notions about the purpose of life, the relationship between the physical

---

8. Nathan Jones, *Sharing the Old, Old Story* (Winona, Minn.: St. Mary's Press, 1982), p. 10.

9. These elements are repeated and expanded as they relate to family catechesis in my article "The Black Family that Is Church" in *Families: Black and Catholic, Catholic and Black,* Sr. Thea Bowman, ed. (Washington, D.C.: USCC Office of Publishing and Promotion Services, 1985), pp. 58-59.

and spiritual, and the role of the transcendent in life. Culture is the natural foundation on which religion must be built. Consequently, successful evangelization and catechesis within the black Catholic community can begin only with a basic reverence, respect, and knowledge of that culture that resides within it.

Revelation needs to be stressed as an essential source for a black articulation in catechesis. Revelation must be understood as the self-disclosure of God in human history, offering communion and salvation for all people who chose to respond in faith. Scripture is the quintessential aspect of revelation, revealing Jesus Christ and his resurrection event, which is the central liberational focus in a catechesis that is addressing appropriately the struggle and suffering inherent in the black experience. Clearly, catechetical leadership for liberation demands constant contemplation of the power and presence of God, who is incarnate in all of creation. Growing awareness of this reality promotes open and respectful dialogue and humility among those who are responsible for leading and teaching in the black community of faith.

4. A Realistic Plan for Action

We need, however, to provide a realistic, feasible plan for action if catechesis is to have a more profound significance and acceptance for the black Catholic community, which is also related to the indigenous traditions of other black Christian churches. We need to offer a rationale for the foundations and the ministry of catechesis that has a black Catholic perspective. Here, it may be helpful to use a conceptual frame of reference to outline somewhat more practically what the components of a black Catholic perspective must include if catechetical leadership is to speak authentically to the life-experience and the faith of black people.

a) First of all, a black articulated catechesis must be offered in conjunction with a black theology that intends to present a world view or a new vision of an entire people. That world view or new vision is the recognition by black people that "we are somebodies"—free, black, beautiful, and proud because we belong above all to God.

b) The agenda of the black community in this country must be reshaped to describe what this "somebodiness" means—individually, collectively, educationally, economically, socially, culturally, and politically. Essentially, this implies humanization of the dehumanized, the liberation of the oppressed, the empowerment of the powerless through the process of evangelization, as well as through worship, as companion pieces to catechesis.

c) Catechesis as a ministry of the Word for black people must express a spirituality related to everyday concerns and realities, making more meaningful in the life of our institutions and in our more intimate living arrangements the conviction that Jesus Christ reigns in the here-and-now as well as in the future he brings upon us.

d) Implicit in any instructional effort oriented toward liberation is the objective of change. There must be the expectation of conversion, of metanoia, of becoming new selves. Catechesis, as a ministry of the Word, fulfills a normative function when it offers "an understanding of the process of social change for justice and new humanity and the necessary struggle, sacrifice, and conflict involved in such change."[10]

e) Catholic educational programs, limited almost exclusively to CCD programs, parochial schools, and sacramental preparation efforts reach only a minority of black youths and adults. A catechesis with a serious liberation component would increase the Church's outreach and mission. Leadership for liberation in the catechetical ministries of education and evangelization calls for a style of ecumenism that transcends the denominational boundaries, which appear to divide the black Christian community.

5. Conclusion

The opening assertion of this essay may serve to summarize the central thrust of its development. Every experience of positive leadership in the black community has been linked inevitably to an expression of liberation and to a theology of hope. These expressions of liberation and the theology of hope, which are articulated and acted out by those who exercise leadership, can only be accepted as authentically indigenous catechesis within the Church if they are developed in dialogue with the black Catholic community, with whom they share mutual responsibility for maintaining the faith. If a central objective of indigenous catechetical ministry is the retelling of the story of God in such a way as to engage a particular people in the recounting of our own collective and individual stories of conversion and communion that follow from this divine revelation, then the categories of reference listed above may serve as a means of evaluating and expanding the effectiveness of catechetical leadership for liberation in the black Catholic community.

---

10. Vincent Harding, "Seven Goals in Education." Talk delivered to an education workshop, Institute of the Black World, Atlanta (May 13, 1973).

Leadership and Professional Development in Light of the Native American Experience

Sr. Genevieve Cuny, OSF

Our first task in approaching another people, another culture, another religion is to take off our shoes, for the place we are approaching is holy. Else we may find ourselves treading on another's dream; and, more serious still, we may forget that God was there before our arrival.

Author Unknown

Before anyone can share the Word of God with native peoples, it is important to have a deep respect for their culture. It is not possible to share catechesis with the native people without an enduring relationship with Jesus. Leadership and professional development in the native way is a different kind of experience. Native formation is much less formal than "business as usual."

The Church, by its very nature, must always and everywhere proclaim and give witness to God's saving love revealed by Jesus Christ in the Holy Spirit. This is the center and foundation of the Church's mission—to proclaim that in Jesus Christ, the Incarnate Word, who died and rose from the dead, salvation is offered to all people as a gift of God's grace and mercy.[1]

This Good News of salvation is not bound by time or human structures. Christ's Gospel of love and redemption, addressed to all

---

1. National Conference of Catholic Bishops, *Statement of U.S. Catholic Bishops on American Indians* (Washington, D.C: USCC Office of Publishing and Promotion Services, 1977), p. 2.

people, transcends national boundaries, cultural differences and divisions among peoples. It cannot be considered identical with any particular culture or heritage.[2]

The Christian faith should celebrate and strengthen the many diverse cultures which are the product of human hope and aspiration. The Gospel message must take root and grow within each culture and each community. Faith finds expression in and through the particular values, customs, and institutions of the people who hear it. It seeks to take flesh within each culture, within each nation, within each race, while remaining the prisoner of none.[3]

Pope Paul VI, in his statement on evangelization, stressed these themes in calling for "fidelity both to a message . . . and to the people to whom it is transmitted."[4]

Culture is an important, but too frequently ignored, source of creativity for the missionary. Just as the economists are discovering that Third World countries need to approach their economic situations through their cultural understandings, it is also clear that a missionary presence must be rooted in the culture of the people. Without that cultural rooting, it is impossible to reflect creatively on the faith. Jesus, throughout the Gospels, sided with the people. He affirmed the wisdom that they had. He used the experiences of their lives to illustrate his stories of the kingdom. The Incarnation itself attests the necessity of entering into, and being part of, culture. The Gospel takes root and shape along the contours of culture.

It is necessary that those who engage in missionary activity, even for a time, should receive a training suited to their condition. These different forms of training should be undertaken in the countries to which they are to be sent, so that the missionary might more fully understand the history, social structures, and customs of the people, that they might have an insight into their moral outlook, their religious precepts and the intimate ideas which they form of God, the world and men according to their own sacred traditions. They should learn their language so that they can speak it easily and correctly and so be able to enter more easily into the minds and hearts of the people.[5]

Enculturation is the process by which an individual absorbs the culture. Everybody learns "right and wrong" from the family, culture, and ex-

2. Ibid.
3. Ibid., p. 3.
4. Ibid.
5. Austin Flannery, OP, ed., "Decree on the Church's Missionary Activity," *Vatican Council II: The Conciliar and Post Conciliar Documents* (Collegeville, Minn.: The Liturgical Press, 1975), no. 26.

periences. In times of crises or tension, our instinctive reaction will be dictated by the cultural traditions. Psychologists call this the *root paradigm*—a pattern of behavior and reaction to a given situation. Every culture has a different root paradigm, which is not necessarily good or a value. Every culture will react differently to life, death, joy, and suffering. The way each culture experiences these factors is different. Know the cultural roots of the tribes to affirm the values and correct any misconceptions. No matter how difficult it might be to live up to the cultural values, there are deficiencies. I experienced a lack of forgiveness in some families among the Lakota people in South Dakota. However, the power of the Gospel can heal these wounds, as Pope John Paul II reminds catechists in his *On Catechesis in Our Time:*

> They are convinced that true catechesis eventually enriches these cultures by helping them to go beyond the defective or even inhuman features in them and by communicating to their legitimate values the fullness of Christ.[6]

The catechist may ask, "How do I get to know the people?" Participation in their community activities and religious ceremonies will build friendships. Firsthand experiences are best. Mutual respectful dialogue is essential. What do native peoples think about the books written about them? What speaks to them? What values are important? Reinforce the beauty already existing. Learn the needs and values of groups. Affirm the goodness in the customs. Purify the limitations.

Enculturation and inculturation—what is the difference? *Enculturation* is reinforcing the values of a culture. *Inculturation* is a process though which, together with the people, one discovers the creative, sanctifying, and liberating action of God in cultural customs and religiosity. It is not a product, but a process through which faith in Jesus becomes the principle of inspiration and action within a culture. Evangelization and inculturation are positively correlated terms.

> We can say of catechesis, as well as of evangelization in general, that it is called to bring the power of the Gospel into the very heart of culture and cultures. For this purpose, catechesis will seek to know these cultures and their essential components; it will learn their most significant expressions; it will be able to offer these cultures the knowledge of the hidden mystery and help them to bring forth from their own living tradition expressions of Christan life, celebration and thought. . . . Genuine catechesis knows that catechesis "takes flesh in the various cultures and milieux. . . ."[7]

6. John Paul II, *Catechist: Text and Commentary on "Catechesi Tradendae"* (Chicago: Franciscan Herald Press, 1980), no. 53.

7. Ibid.

Find Jesus in the culture. Gospel values are already present. The person and message of Jesus have been alive for thousands of years, but often the tribes did not know the name and power of the message. Native ways are generally gospel ways, but they need to be identified, explored, and embraced. In this way, the deficiencies, lack, and shortcomings will be revealed. Where is God for the native people? Whom do they say Jesus is? It is important to absorb the cultural aspects in the celebration of the sacraments. How does the catechist do it? First, celebrate. Then, celebrate the reality of life in the liturgy.

By using the cross-cultural approach, the missionary allows the inculturation to happen. This implies a knowledge of one another's history, mutual listening, and learning. Each culture needs to recognize the difference between the realities of its religious faith and the cultural expressions of these realities. It means that each culture must demythologize the essential elements of its belief system in order to share the basic realities with other cultures. Each culture needs to reflect continuously on the realities of faith in prayerful searching of the sacred to find ways to express these realities in their richest language, symbol, and cultural forms. By mutually searching out the sacred, each culture heightens its own awareness of how the spiritual presence is manifested through its own symbols and sacramental forms.[8]

Who are to become catechists? Pope John Paul II states, "All are to become catechists, yes, including most explicitly the laity. But they are to be carefully prepared. This should be self-evident since this task is, at the very least, of great importance to the Church."[9]

What is the true meaning of this preparation? Pope John Paul II does not see this as a "formally instituted ministry." He says, "What is needed is not another echelon of officials, but rather a corps of effective workers in the field."[10] But to get such workers, some effective preparation is necessary; for this, he sees the need of "special centers and institutes."

The native people have just such a center. The Tekakwitha Conference is an annual gathering of Catholic Indians from the United States and Canada to share and celebrate the native and Catholic traditions. Its national headquarters are located in Great Falls, Montana. The Conference has sponsored summer institutes for the orientation of people in ministry with native peoples since 1982. Since 1979, the Conference has included the area of catechesis in each of its annual meetings. During the summer of 1985, three native catechists developed goals, objectives, and a course of study for the formation of native catechists. For the first time

---

8. Gilbert F. Hemauer, "A Cross-Cultural Approach to Catechesis among Native Americans," *The Living Light* 14:1 (Spring 1977): 134.

9. *John Paul II, Catechist,* no. 77.

10. Ibid.

in the history of the Catholic Church among native Americans, two native catechists presented an outline of catechetical study for native catechists to a group of nonnatives who were attending the annual summer institute in Great Falls, Montana. Beginning in 1986, a native catechesis workshop will be offered each summer in different geographical areas of the United States. The Archbishop Cousins Catholic Center in Milwaukee will be the site for this year's workshop. The workshops focus on the native catechists' personal experiences of Jesus in the light of their native experiences.

Sharing the Light of Faith: National Catechetical Directory for Catholics of the United States gives specific guidelines for dealing with cultural, racial, and ethnic groups.

First, it is necessary to distinguish subgroups (e.g., Mexican Americans, Puerto Ricans, Cubans, and immigrants from other Latin American countries, even Spain itself). Similarly, one must be aware of the various tribes and nations of native Americans.[11]

Following that, the catechists will be members of the groups; but if this is not possible, they should understand the people and empathize with their needs.[12] Be open to listen to the native people in the way they wish to catechize. For an example, while I was working on the Rosebud Indian Reservation in southcentral South Dakota, I became familiar with the home religion program. It was already in place when I arrived. After a couple of months' experience in the home program, a catechist suggested that periodically we gather as groups of families and share the faith. These gatherings or clusters were based on relationships, not on geographic areas. Relatives as well as friends were welcome to come. This draws upon the experiences of life.

Here is the third guideline: They should know the language of the group, "not just its vocabulary, but its thought patterns, cultural idioms, customs, and symbols."[13] Abstract thought or ideologies alone do not communicate to people who move with the heart.

Another guideline: The catechist should be sensitive to "catechetical materials, especially in translating and adapting materials prepared for others, so that pictures as well as text affirm the identity and dignity of the members of the particular group.[14] Some do not do this. There is a standstill in catechetical materials suitable for native peoples. The people will no longer accept the same materials as those used by nonnative catechists.

---

11. *Sharing the Light of Faith: National Catechetical Directory for Catholics of the United States* (Washington, D.C.: USCC Office of Publishing and Promotion Services, 1979), no. 194.
12. Ibid.
13. Ibid.
14. Ibid.

In this same reference, catechists are reminded, catechesis takes into account the education and economic resources and the particular efforts of ethnic groups to "obtain, keep, or exercise their rights."[15]

Continuing, *Sharing the Light of Faith* sees the need for multicultural catechesis even in areas and parishes that are homogenous: "All should be educated to know and respect other cultural, racial, and ethnic groups, avoiding condescension and patronizing attitudes."[16]

While ministering in a border town on the Rosebud Reservation in South Dakota, I found the Lakota people to be the dominant group. I respected both the Lakota culture and the non-Indian culture but ministered strongly with the Lakota people. This included accommodating the non-Indians. History tells us that some of the early missionaries did not operate this way. Could this be one of the reasons for the lack of religious and priestly vocations from among native peoples?

Finally, the Church at large is called upon to "make a special commitment to provide funds, research, materials, and personnel for catechesis directed to ethnic groups."[17] The ultimate aim is to help cultural, racial, and ethnic groups to provide for their own catechetical needs. I believe the native people are ready and willing to assume these responsibilities but are often unsure about what to do. These dedicated people need recognition, affirmation, support, and training to contribute to the faith life of their communities.

Catechist formation is seen from a ministerial point of view instead of just meeting the standards. When catechesis is seen as a ministry—a vocation—the requirements for this ministry become necessary steps to prepare oneself for serving God's people. Good catechist programs include "those [programs] which are designed to develop personal faith as well as each of the specific qualities and competencies that enables the catechist to place theological content at the service of effective catechesis."[18] This call is not to a bookish, heady professionalism but to faith response with knowledge and experience.

It is essential that catechists take time to learn more about the faith they want to share and about the art of sharing it personally and effectively. The response to the call of being a catechist includes "willingness to give time and talent, not only to catechizing others, but to one's own continued growth in faith and understanding."[19]

Becoming a catechist is not a matter of learning how to do something *to* others, nor is it learning how to do something *for* others. Rather, it is

---

15. Ibid.

16. Ibid.

17. Ibid.

18. Robert J. Hater, *Parish Catechetical Ministry: A Resource of the National Conference of Diocesan Directors of Religious Education* (Encino, Calif.: Glencoe Publishing Co., 1986), p. 66.

19. *Sharing the Light of Faith*, no. 206.

learning how to do something *with* others. The emphasis is on relationship. The catechist is seen as a witness to and a prophet of the message communicated.

Catechists can build these relationships only as they become trained properly to communicate sensitively the gospel message to the unique situation of the group or individual they address:

> The summit and center of catechetical formation lies in an aptitude and ability to communicate the gospel message. This formation requires, therefore, an accurate formation in theological doctrine, in anthropology, and in methodology, geared to the level of knowledge that is to be attained. The formation does not end, however, with the acquisition of doctrinal knowledge. The formation is complete when the catechist becomes competent to select the most suitable method for communicating the gospel message to groups and individuals who live in circumstances always different and singular.[20]

To speak of native catechists is to speak of peer catechetics. There is definitely no tidy organized method. The person must feel the call to be a catechist, must be mature, and must know her or his environment. The person should be respected by the community and be willing to examine his or her motives for teaching. The preparation of the catechist should be slow—at the person's own speed—and organized carefully.

The catechists need to be catechized in the native American way. The Church must be humble enough, as Church, to ask the people to do this. The native people will be the teachers. The emphasis should be on experience rather than ideas. Ways must be found to pass on stories, sacred ways—the best of native tradition and the tradition of the Catholic Church.

The native catechists themselves will identify with the stories (native tradition and the Gospel) and share these values with the learning non-native catechists, as well as with others. They will speak of the sacred places to help others understand.

Here are some teaching principles, pedagogical ways of entering and sharing native American cultures:

- Use oral tradition, primarily storytelling, as the natural vehicle of instruction. This is a natural, exciting, and memorable way.
- Experience realities by personal presence in the family, tribe, and sacred ceremonies as the ordinary manner of learning. This is the best way to come to know the people to form friendships.
- Understand that traditional ways require leaders to give instructions. These leaders will let one know what and when to do things.

---

20. Vatican Sacred Congregation for the Clergy, *General Catechetical Directory* (Washington, D.C.: USCC Office of Publishing and Promotion Services, 1977), no. 111.

- Respect older people teaching younger people. This is counter-culture, but needs to be maintained and restored.
- Know that every culture has its etiquette in communication. It is necessary to know and respect the differences.
- Take advantage of clear pictorial expressions that communicate best. Abstractions and theory may cloud the teachings.
- Remember native peoples live in a close relationship with the Creator. A religion of words alone is foreign to the people.
- Catechize in such a way that it reflects the values, traditions, and customs of the tribes. This comes easily out of gospel values.
- Take time to listen to the elders (men and women) of the tribes to relearn, rediscover, reinforce their values. These are strengths that will be handed down to the next generation.
- Seek out the tribes' storytellers and learn their history, traditions, and customs. This is a source of pride for the people.
- Study and pray the holy Scriptures. This deepens the faith experience in relation to tribal history.
- Explore spiritual insights God has given to the tribes. Ask what Christian teachings can be added or developed.
- Integrate cultural values in religious education programs. This catechesis offers new experiences for the tribes as well as the missionaries.
- Turn to the gifts of creation as easy meditation for tribal people. Use them as tools for family gatherings.
- Stress and affirm these native traditions. Awake to creation, reverence, respect, and generosity. Challenge what seems to deny the best in them: harshness toward and neglect of children; choosing the way of noise and speed; and not passing on the most sacred values. This affirmation has helped others to be sensitive and to listen, no matter what the environment. This will make it possible for catechesis to happen.

Making it possible for native peoples to catechize is part of the renewal of catechetics Pope John Paul II talks about in his exhortation on *Catechesis in Our Time*. It must be done with what the pope calls "an attitude of faith." The catechetical enterprise itself must be based on faith. The pope recalls, "an attitude of faith always has reference to the faithfulness of God, who never fails to respond."[21]

Drawing on the two themes of culture and faith . . . , we hope to fashion a renewed commitment to serve Indian people. . . . In turn, their participation in and challenge to our Christian community will strengthen our common witness to Jesus and the gospel message.[22]

---

21. *John Paul II, Catechist*, no. 15.
22. *Statement of U.S. Catholic Bishops on American Indians*, p. 9.

Leadership and professional development will bring life's total experience into the words and the teachings of the native catechist. As Pope John Paul II says, "the person who lives out a catechesis is the best catechist."

The native catechist must keep asking: What are the sources of our faith? How are the older people our resources? How can the native way of meeting death help all of us today? How can we help the young search for what is holy? How can we help them examine their values? How, together, are we to eat and pray and dance and give away?

III. Program Development

Toward the Fulfillment of a Dream
Sr. María de la Cruz Aymes, SH

An Afro-American Perspective
Nathan Jones, Ph.D.

Program Development and Native American Catechesis
Sr. Kateri Mitchell, SSA

Toward the Fulfillment of a Dream

Sr. María de la Cruz Aymes, SH

The thunderous applause at the conclusion of the *III Encuentro Nacional Hispano de Pastoral* left no doubt that the Hispanic people were at the threshold of a new era in their history in the United States. They had culminated their intensive diocesan and regional preparation with a vision of their mission in the Catholic Church of America. With prophetic voice, they enunciated pastoral guidelines and made public commitments to implement them.

It rained on that closing day. But far from dampening the spirits, the water was like a sign that the seeds of hope in a new future would be abundantly watered by the gifts of the Holy Spirit. That rain was also symbolic of the laborious stage of cultivation, during which the dreams the Encuentro had created would materialize, take hold, deepen their roots, and spread throughout the land.

The Encuentro was the fruit of a massive communal effort; so will be the implementation of its vision. Local and diocesan meetings are taking place across the country; the already established NCCB/USCC Secretariat for Hispanic Affairs, regional offices, and Catholic Hispanic institutes are working to develop programs for a *pastoral de conjunto*—a master pastoral plan. Every word, every action is needed to achieve the dream. Every bit counts!

And, here is one of those "bits"—another drop of rain on a field pregnant with new life. The purpose of this paper is not to repeat the proposals, commitments, and pastoral guidelines developed during the Encuentro (these are contained in *Prophetic Voices*, available from USCC Office of Publishing and Promotion Services) but to explore some practical ways of implementing, at the parish and grass-roots levels, the challenges raised by the Encuentro.

While the Hispanic people have the right to expect help from the institutional Church to respond to their request, the fact remains, "God

helps those who help themselves"— "*A Dios rogando y con el mazo dando.*"
It is in proportion to our giving that we will receive. It would be wrong
to put off what could be done already. If the Hispanic people take the
initiative at the local level, get organized, and work to attain what they
have a right to, those in authority will be moved to back their efforts and
give them support and assistance.

Due to the limited scope of this article, only six pastoral guidelines
will be touched. However, it is hoped that it will stimulate the creativity
of Hispanics in their parishes and motivate them to continue the thrust
of evangelization, education, and social justice initiated by the Encuentro.
These three elements are essential to the fulfillment of their mission, and
must inspire the desire to (1) increase their love and knowledge of God
and their Catholic faith; (2) develop their own human talents and cultural
potentials; (3) assist them to obtain their rights so that they can live with
dignity, in peace and security, and in better circumstances.

1. "We, as Hispanic people, want to develop and follow a pastoral de conjunto that responds to our reality."

Practical Suggestions

a) To work toward a local pastoral plan, every parish should have an
Hispanic pastoral committee or council. This committee could be organized or revitalized by the pastor with grass-roots volunteers or with an
active *Comunidad de Base*. The committee should be composed of men
and women, youths and adults, singles and marrieds, representing different Hispanic backgrounds. From the onset, they should use all the
elements for the formation of a Basic Ecclesial Community: prayer, scrip-
tural reflection, communal discernment for goal setting, decision making,
and evaluation.

b) The first task of the committee is to conduct a door-to-door survey
in order to make contact and get to know every Hispanic family in the
parish. Even if some data is already available in the parish records, in all
probability updated information would be lacking, especially in areas
where there are many Hispanics who are migrants, poor, undocumented,
and who do not speak English or who have left the Church. The purposes
of the survey are to get to know the real situation of Hispanics in the
parish; enter into direct communication with the people; surface and name
their needs and potentials; motivate and coordinate ministries for and by
Hispanics; develop leadership, stimulating education; and bring back to
the Catholic Church those who have left it.

This central task of the committee—to know the people and their
needs—corresponds to one of the fundamental principles in evangeliza-

tion: education and social justice. Knowledge is here used in its full biblical dimension, including love and respect for each person; it goes beyond gathering ordinary data such as name, age, address, and occupation. As messengers of Christ, we have to be open to the hopes, fears, joys, and concerns of the people. We have to learn to appreciate what they value: their culture, family traditions and customs, their language and religiosity. We must know what their needs are, both material and spiritual, and also their gifts and potentials to enrich the community. This knowledge requires dialogue. Only when mutual trust is established and there is a genuine sense of friendship and partnership, can one begin to truly communicate with and get to know a person.

c) Home visitations of Hispanics by Hispanic leaders are essential.

(1) Set a date for initiation of the survey and spread the news of its purpose through notices, pulpit announcements, and word-of-mouth.

(2) Make a phone call to Hispanic families registered in the parish records to set a convenient time for the first visit. Inquire if some young members of the family might be willing to help in the survey. Invite them to come to the training session(s) for the survey.

(3) Prepare two types of questionnaires: a general one for the whole family living at the same address, and an individual one for each member of the family, including each child. (See suggestions at the end of this article.)

(4) At the planning/training session, have an enlarged map of the parish and divide it into sectors, as it is done for any survey. Appoint a "sector coordinator" and assign to him or her a given number of workers. Their addresses and telephone numbers should be listed so they can keep in touch during the survey.

(5) As a group, and preferably with the assistance of a professional organizer, decide on the approach to be used: plan on making two or even three calls to establish rapport with the family; have a distinctive badge with the name of the parish; dress in a way acceptable to the people; always make the calls in pairs and in a friendly way.

(6) At the first visit, they are to introduce themselves, explain the purpose of the survey, read the questions in the cards, and leave the forms to be completed. Set a time for the team to return to talk with them about the survey, preferably at a time when more members of the family are gathered. Explain that the team will then help them in writing out the answers.

(7) On the second visit, plan to learn more about the family. Begin with a short prayer: the Our Father and/or Hail Mary. The visitors should then tell the family a bit about themselves: where they live; how long they have been in the neighborhood; what they enjoy about the Church; what programs they would want to see established in the parish. Open the way to dialogue by pointing out some of the obvious needs of Hispanics in the area of evangelization, education, and social justice. Ask for the

family's opinions of these matters, as well as their ideas of what could be done in general; take note of what they say. Then, proceed with filling out the information sheets. Conclude with a prayer for the intentions of the family and the success of the survey.

2. "We, as Hispanic people, want to follow the pastoral approach of promoting Hispanic leadership that is incarnated and committed."

Practical Suggestions

a) The committee should seek resources in pastoral planning to train its members to set goals and objectives, based on the reality of the local situation revealed by the survey; categorize and prioritize needs and match them with potentials; practice the art of addressing people, conducting group discussions, and organizing and coordinating programs; develop awareness of the importance of attitude, body language, and tone of voice, without sounding patronizing or dictatorial. The evangelical dimension of their leadership should be stressed. Their attitude in their contact with the people should be that of a messenger of Christ, whose reason for finding out who and where Hispanics are, is to "serve" them in their needs, to better their situation, and to help them develop their potentials and mature as children of God.

b) The parish Hispanic committee has to assume a role of leadership in planning and carrying out a *pastoral de conjunto*. This implies having a clear vision of the goals and concrete means to respond to the needs of the people and winning the trust of the parishioners. The members of the committee are to give witness of a true Christian community, where prayer, mutual respect, and teamwork are possible. It should be open to and welcome the input of parish associations that are functioning already in the parish. The committee is not to work in competition with them; true leadership calls for the ability to work in collaboration with others, recognizing the service they are already doing and affirming it.

c) In its leadership capacity, the committee has the responsibility to raise funds for the implementation of the pastoral plan. The "formation to leadership," requested by the Encuentro, will begin to take place as the Hispanics take the initiative to assume their responsibilities. Fund raising can be organized using time-honored means to get the people to work together.

(1) Organize a *Feria Cultural Hispana.* Invite all Hispanics in the parish to take part in a cultural talent show: native songs, folklore dances, foods, displays of ethnic costumes, and even sale of arts and crafts. The parish school staff may be willing to collaborate. Assign different aspects of the fair to different groups: youths in charge of publicity; couples to coordinate

68

the program; men responsible for the admission fee and general order; women to prepare food to be sold; children to decorate, making banners and favors to be sold. Attract participants with prizes, which could consist of objects donated for that purpose; offer door prizes; and so forth.

(2) Have a "Pre-Cana and Cana Dance," organized by members of the Christian Family Movement or Encuentro.

(3) Offer a traditional "Hispanic Food Fair," with food donated by neighborhood restaurants that can use the event as publicity.

(4) Give a report on the funds raised and how they are to be used.

d) Once trained in the basics of leadership, the members of the committee could form "specialized pastoral teams," with three to five of their members responsible for a given aspect of the parish pastoral plan. For example: catechetics and integral education; the family and women; youths; the poor and social justice. The pastoral teams, in turn, should enlist the help of other Hispanics in the parish who know the culture and needs of the people, have some experience in that particular field, or are willing to be trained. Important members of the Hispanic community, *barrio*, or *vecindad* should be consulted. Key persons are not only the elders in the family but also the local barber and hairdresser, the neighborhood drugstore clerk, the pharmacist, the vendors at the marketplace who know the ways of the people and have their trust. The importance of enlisting persons from different ethnic groups and even socioeconomic levels should be evident. They can name the real concerns and needs of the people.

3. "We, as Hispanic people, want to follow a line of integral education sensitive to our cultural identity."

Knowledge and education are keys to freedom at all levels. Ignorance of who we are and the inability to develop our potentials are forms of oppression. Education is a way to liberation. To be truly free, people need to know how to protect their rights and fulfill their responsibilities to themselves and to the community.

Practical Suggestions

a) The committee should get information from the diocesan or regional offices for Hispanics and find out what courses are being offered by the parochial and public schools in the area. This information should be made known to Hispanics, who very often are not aware of what is available or need motivation to study. If specific fields of needed education are not being offered, the pastor should be asked to help find instructors to give intensive courses of short duration. This is important. It is easier to find volunteers to give a limited number of classes, and students who have been away from classrooms will more likely attend them. Once they develop a taste for learning and sense its benefits, they will enroll more readily in more extensive studies.

b) Courses or workshops offered should be publicized widely and be of immediate enrichment, enjoyment, and practical benefit. For example:

Spanish literacy tutoring classes. Many Hispanics did not have the opportunity to learn how to read and write in their own language.

English literacy tutoring classes. Knowledge of English is crucial. Many young Hispanics drop out of school or do not find better working positions because of their inability to speak, read, and write English. They and their parents need help and incentive to be bilingual.

Religious education in Spanish. Formation of Hispanic catechists; bilingual catechetical classes for all age levels; adaptation of the RCIA program for Hispanics; essentials of our Catholic faith, vs. fundamentalism; Scripture and basic apologetics to help resist the inroads of sects are all needed.

Trade and apprenticeship workshops. Hispanics are very gifted in many trades and crafts but often lack the basic knowledge of how to get started. Parishioners who already have a trade could be asked to volunteer four to six hours to teach the fundamentals in plumbing, carpentry, hairdressing, cooking, sewing, gardening, and so forth.

Cultural workshops. Due to circumstances, Hispanics, especially young ones, are often deprived of an environment that makes them proud of their culture. They have lost contact with their cultural roots. They do not know the history of their people, the stories and legends that inspire their folklore, the arts and crafts characteristic of their country. They are culturally illiterate. Workshops could provide ways and means for them to discover their own talents and cultural inclinations through dance, plastic arts, music, drama, and ethnic folklore.

Civic and legal counseling. Many Hispanics, whether they are documented or not are ignorant of their rights and do not know where to go for help in legal matters. Among the parishioners, find a lawyer or knowledgeable person who would hold an occasional "open forum" for Hispanics to tell them what kind of help they need, where they can find it, and to answer their questions.

Even if, at first, these courses and/or workshops are not well attended because of lack of publicity or mistrust of the people, efforts should be sustained. They can becoame an invaluable service to Hispanics, especially the poor.

4. "We, as Hispanic people, choose the family in all its expressions as the core of our pastoral ministry."

The Hispanic family, as a whole, should be approached rather than individuals. The extended family—grandparents, parents, children, uncles, aunts, cousins—embodies the most important values for Hispanics: their language, their culture, their faith. It constitutes their real "social security." Family obligations and hospitality are fundamental in the Hispanic culture. Poorer or newly arrived relatives are sure to find a home among *la familia*, and the receiving household will go to extremes to make them feel welcome, even at the expense of their own welfare. Family obligations have top priority, and supersede the need for education or even parish duties. *La familia viene primero.*

Practical Suggestions

a) Involve the elders in the family. Most Hispanic families have members of older generations living at home. Often, grandmothers are the baby sitters and the transmitters of cultural religiosity, family customs, and traditions. They might be illiterate and know very little English, but they are responsible for the education of the little chidlren. To win the trust of the grandparents is to open the doors to the whole family. Even if, at first, they will be hesitant to speak, grandmothers are the best suited to give information regarding the members of the household.

b) Address the whole family in parish notices. The whole family should always be invited and included in parish celebrations, projects, or events, not just the children and parents.

c) Affirm the religious customs of the family. The religiosity practiced at home keeps alive the faith of Hispanics. Due to many factors in their history, such as religious and political persecutions, dearth of priests, and great distance from the church, many Hispanic families developed the habit of praying in the privacy of their homes. Hence, the traditional family shrine, the *altarcito*, with a variety of holy images and colorfully decorated. It is before this shrine that the family gathers to pray. These family devotions are often more satisfying to Hispanics than the parish liturgies celebrated in a language and style foreign to their culture.

The perception of the type of religiosity practiced by different Hispanic groups should be brought to the attention of the pastor, the liturgical commission, and religious educators. Knowledge and understanding of what speaks to and nourishes the faith of people is crucial for their ongoing religious education.

5. "We, as Hispanic people, wish to follow an approach of valuing and promoting women, recognizing their equality and dignity and their role in the Church, the family, and society."

Without a doubt, it is due to the influence of Hispanic women that their culture and language have survived in this country. They are the ones who provide the environment where enculturation takes place. But, Hispanic women face a double burden at home and in society. Culturally, they are dominated by the *machismo* of their husbands, who make heavy demands on them, and often face alone the responsibility of educating the children; their "equality" consists in having to work to help support the family. Hispanic women are drained and have little opportunity to better their education. Though some are struggling for greater freedom, the feminist movement still runs counter-culture, and many Hispanic women are too tired to struggle for their rights both at home and in society. The working Hispanic woman is often caught in the drudgery of menial work, in the fields, factories or as maids, which offers scant remuneration and no retirement security. It is love for their family that gives them courage to go on.

Practical Suggestions

a) Utilize a multifaceted approach to help Hispanic women.

(1) The Hispanic committee should find out what public and Catholic services are available to help women with their needs, whether it be battered wives, single mothers, or women wanting education but unable to afford it. The services offered by these organizations should be publicized in Spanish at regular intervals.

(2) Workshops and/or short courses could be offered in the parish in Spanish, not only on topics that young housewives might need, such as child care, nutrition, physical and mental hygiene, English, Spanish, etc., but also provide for recreational and educational workshops: music, dance, art, typing, aerobics.

(3) Provide baby-sitting service for mothers who need to attend school. This could be done by organizing a network among the Hispanic community. Some mothers or grandmothers who already are baby-sitting their own children might be willing to take care of another child.

b) Recognize the role of Hispanic women in the Church.

(1) Establish the custom of having an annual "Recognition Day" for all the women who volunteer their services in the parish, including the cook, the housekeeper, and the secretary. At a Sunday Mass, call them to receive a visible sign of appreciation: a corsage, a medal, or a plaque.

(2) Make public mention of and congratulate professional Hispanic women in the parish who hold important positions and offer public services in the city. This is an incentive to other women to study and better themselves.

(3) Have an annual dinner for all women volunteers: catechists, choir members, lectors, altar society members, etc. It would be a fine touch if this dinner were planned and served by the men in the parish, including the parish priests.

6. "We, as Hispanic people, make a preferential option for Hispanic youths, so that they will participate at all levels of pastoral ministry."

The greatest challenge to the Hispanic committee is to provide support and guidance to the youths of the parish, being aware of the pressures and crises they are going through—psychological, cultural, and religious. Many Hispanic youths are dropouts who, out of fear or to satisfy their need for identity, join gangs and use drugs. Many no longer come near the church nor any Catholic institution. But, in every parish there are a few young people who are searching for the values of their faith and culture. Precisely because they are few in number, they should not be neglected. It is imperative to involve them in the formulation and implementation of the parish pastoral plan.

Practical Suggestions

a) Have youth representatives as members of the Hispanic committee.

b) Invite them to take part in the parish survey. Direct contact with the needs of families will be educational and trigger their creativity and initiative.

c) Give them a leadership role in parish events, keeping in mind that youths will respond better if the task is defined clearly.

d) Urge the liturgy commission to invite Hispanic youths to participate in visible roles such as ushers, readers, choir members, acolytes; give them a distinctive symbol of their ministry to wear: a medal or a badge.

e) Train teenagers and young adults to help in the catechetical programs for younger children, beginning as teacher's aides and gradually assuming the role of catechists.

f) Entrust them to form groups of "service to seniors": visiting homes for the aged; escorting them to do their shopping; reading to them, etc. For their own security, it is always recommended that they offer these services in pairs.

It is evident that not everything can be done at once. Communal discernment has to be used to decide which programs have top priority because of the urgency of the needs discovered during the survey. What matters is to begin now, locally, sowing the mustard seed or revitalizing what was dropped in the past because of apparent "lack of success." The real failure is to give up or to be frightened by the magnitude of the task. The harvest is ready—and Christ is with the laborers who have the courage and generosity to begin to plow the field.

We move on toward the fulfillment of a dream as Hispanic believers.

SAMPLE SURVEY

[On the outside of a 6" × 9" manila envelope, print the following:]

I. GENERAL FAMILY INFORMATION

Family Name _____

Address _____ Telephone _____

Family's Country of Origin _____

Approximate Length of Time in the United States _____

Family's Religion _____

Number of Family Members Currently Living at This Address _____

Most Urgent Need or Concern _____

Date of Survey _____ Names of Visitors _____

[On Side 1 of 5½" × 8½" cards, which go into the envelope, print:]

II. PERSONAL INFORMATION

First Name _____

Father's Full Name _____

Mother's Full Name _____

Relationship to Family _____

Place and Date of Birth _____

Sacraments Received _____ Date _____

_____ Date _____

_____ Date _____

Parish or Church Attended _____

[On Side 2 of the cards, print:]

School Attended _____ Where _____

Highest Grade _____ Reads/Writes Spanish _____

Reads/Writes English _____

Work/Occupation _____

Would Like to Learn = (Mark an "X")   Would Like to Tutor = (Mark a ✔)

Read/Write English ☐   Read/Write Spanish ☐   Guitar ☐   Typing ☐

Carpentry ☐   Cooking ☐   Sewing ☐   Hairdressing ☐

Further Education Needed/Wanted _____

Desire To Be Involved in _____

Most Urgent Need/Concern _____

[These questions could be completed by the parish visitors in dialogue with the family members.]

An Afro-American Perspective

Nathan Jones, Ph.D.

When planning catechetical programs for Afro-American adults, youths, and children, we must necessarily build upon the inherent strengths of the people. Blacks, because of our history, have come to expect certain things from our religion that other persons may not.

Catholic educators generally fail to unravel the marvels of black cultural styles and behaviors. We prefer to insist on rigid conformity to white monocultural teaching/learning styles and act as if blacks were simply "black-skinned whites."

Our starting point in program development will be to acknowledge Afro-Americans as richly endowed. The untrained eye tends to overlook these qualities, underrate their significance, and insist on standard, white middle-class norms. Given the national tendency to view cultural differences as suggestive of inferiority, pastoral leaders are frustrated continuously by low attendance, passivity, and a general lack of interest in parish religious education programs.

This has been said before. We must ask ourselves the following critical questions: What is God asking of us now and in the future? What educational program, then, is required? What are the principal stumbling blocks to effective implementation of culturally appropriate catechetical designs?

Building upon Black Cultural Strengths

Learning takes place in a wide arena in black communities: family, relations, streets, institutions, media, music, and so forth. A broad spectrum of agencies shape the lives and values and determine the behavior and commitment of people. Normally, religious educators neglect to take these learning environments seriously. We fail to acknowedge what the community already provides by way of value formation, rituals, and optimal mental and spiritual health.

Program development begins by examining the distinctive ways black people display the courage to be themselves, to display their own style and unique characteristics. In short, catechists must rigorously study culture, black expressive styles, and behaviors if we are to ever reverse the pattern of sterile, repetitive, and maladaptive religious education modalities that simply don't work.

The study of culture is not a single act, but a process. Films, study texts, guest speakers, field trips, and listening are a means to the end. Here are some questions to guide your inquiry: (1) What are the espoused goals, values, and norms of your local community (2) What are the practiced realities, values, and norms of this community? (3) What are the personal and community behaviors that support the community goals? (4) What are the behaviors that deviate from these goals? (5) How might these behaviors be brought into line with community goals? (6) Who are the key players and carriers of the culture? (7) How are the community's values and norms related to transcendent and Christian values?

Frequently, our ways of ministering are at odds with black styles. Uninitiated educators normally view black culturally specific styles and behaviors with a great deal of suspicion and misunderstanding such as the open expression of feelings; self-glorification; braggadocio in words and body language; coined interjections; loud colors; the use of profanity; and the deliberate violations of structured English syntax.

Educators, guided by the American ethos, prefer to emphasize the rationalistic, repress sexuality, and deny suffering. Conversely, black styles are marked by considerable feeling and movement: a refusal to deodorize life; a resistance to formality and sameness; a comfort with the body, its shape, drives, and scars.

Either style can be, at times, dysfunctional. Therefore, catechists must make an objective appraisal of cultural styles based on the people's needs and community goals. One of the aims of catechesis is to bring the community to an awareness of its own God-given strengths, to reverse negative programming, and to draw religion out of the people rather than pump religion into them.

Pastoral and educational leaders cannot afford to be information-poor. We need to be aware of the context of our learners' lives, use it appropriately, and reflect on it deliberately. Jesus taught in the context of people's lives. He pointed them back to their own experience: farming, relationships, banquets. He invited them to grow and change in the context of their own lives.

Program Imperatives

The following elements are regarded widely as foundational for religious education in black communities: a sense of self, a sense of history, a sense of community, a sense of disciplined growth, and a sense of the sacred. These elements designate key assumptions that programs typically enflesh. An evaulation of your existing program—its philosophy and approaches—is a starter. The aim is not only to order new teaching aids but to understand the need for systemic change in our whole catechetical concept and its interrelated parts. By paying close attention to these imperatives, you can design effective programs, curricula, and select appropirate resources.

1. A Sense of Self

The development of a healthy identity is endemic to catechesis. It involves freeing people from forces (inner/outer) that prevent them from moving toward their full potential.

- Does the program foster self-esteem?
- How does the program aid the search for cultural identity?
- How does the program confront the learner with what it means to be a black Catholic-Christian in America?

2. A Sense of History

We are never isolated from our past or future, although some Christians find it easier to ignore their history than to examine it. History invites us to dream not only of what *has* been but what has *not yet* been. Now that we are driving the bus, where is the bus going?

- Does the program foster an appreciation of Africa as motherland? Afro-American heritage?
- Are students urged to search history to discover ways of making their own personal contribution?
- Does the program include truthful and relevant black content (saints, freedom fighters, liberation movements, arts)?

3. A Sense of Community

The black community is comprised of a repository of natural talent. Look for positive role models among the successful businesspersons, parents, law enforcement officers, reformed offenders, artists, and activists.

- Does the program recognize and engage the talent of the larger community?

4. A Sense of Disciplined Growth

Allowing blacks to think of themselves only as "victims" stigmatizes and further impedes the quest for affirmation and liberation. Challenge prevailing practices such as crime, recreational sex, eating disorders, severe dependency on artificial stimuli, the dissolution of the family, and so forth. Stress *development* rather than simply *survival* mentalities.

- Does the program motivate learners to examine their attitudes and behavior while comprehending their responsibilities?

5. A Sense of the Sacred

Build upon the ability of many blacks to feel deeply and express their feelings without reserve, to relax and enjoy everything they do. Educators who insist on formality and control can suppress affectivity and psycho-motor expressions. Boredom is a direct response to the excessively low activity level of many classrooms. Handclaps, yells of approval, panto-mime, hugs, linked arms, nonverbal cues, hot colors, movement, and rhythms are cultural avenues to the Divine. The absence of words in much of black communication signifies a very healthy readiness for the sacramental—expressing outwardly what we feel inside. Feeling and faith belong together.

- Does the program draw upon the spiritual insights of the people (stories, folk wisdom, songs)?
- Does the program seek to enable blacks to be at home with Catholic tradition and bring to the tradition black gifts and insights?

Conclusion

Answers to these questions for multicultural catechesis are not easy and are never fully satisfied by simple solutions—a gospel choir, a red/black/green altar covering. Maturity mobilizes us to generate a plan for local black church development, that is, total pastoral renewal. Looking backwards, we affirm that past practices and programs were helpful but also limiting. Today, we must move beyond routine and yesterday's agenda. The bishops of the Church have given us the "Go!" signal. It's all up to us!

Program Development and Native American Catechesis

Sr. Kateri Mitchell, SSA

The gospel message, the presence of Jesus, is becoming more real and active in the lives of many peoples who reflect on their personal histories and spiritual journeys in a multicultural circle of faith. Therefore, how does one share a faith that is personal, relevant, vibrant and, at the same time, transforming? John Paul II gives us some direction in this matter. As he states,

> . . . catechesis, is called to bring the power of the Gospel into the very heart of culture and cultures. For this purpose, catechesis will seek to know these cultures and their essential components; it will learn their significant expressions; it will be able to offer these cultures the knowledge of the hidden mystery and help them to bring forth from their own living tradition original expressions of Christian life, celebration, and thought.[1]

Pope John Paul II's catechetical approach presents certain challenges to us. First, we will need to use our peoples' native languages. This means not only vocabulary but cultural idioms, symbols, and thought patterns. Second, it will not be sufficient merely to adapt other catechetical materials for use in our native communities. We will need to develop new materials that will affirm and challenge our native people's traditions and culture.

Let us address the necessity for catechesis development for native people. A native catechesis is an attempt to help us Indian people root ourselves in a deeper understanding of gospel values through our lived experiences of our own tribal stories, languages, family and community

---

1. *John Paul II, Catechist: Text and Commentary on "Catechesi Tradendae"* (Chicago: Franciscan Herald Press, 1980), no. 53.

orientation, values, customs, traditions, symbols, rituals and sacred ceremonies, dances, art, and legends. In fact, the total expression of who we are as individuals and as members of a given Indian tribe, nation, or clan creates a religious experience unique to us as Indian people. Essentially, in designing a relevant and inspirational catechesis, the whole person needs to be considered.

It is, therefore, indispensable to note the identifiable characteristics of a native person. First, the native way of thinking and reasoning is cyclic; that is, one goes around and around using concrete examples and stories before getting to the heart of the issue at hand. Second, three methods of communicating are particular to us: (1) in verbal expression, the concreteness of the language used depicts a visual and earthy style that is descriptive; (2) in nonverbal language, inner feelings and intuitions are transmitted with great effectiveness; (3) in silence, a deep sense of contemplation is communicated.

As we further consider points of development in catechesis, we focus on the discovery of one's personal truths centered on kinship and real life events in our communities.

> By respecting, understanding and accepting the truth about myself, my family, my tribe, the earth and the places where I live, the people I meet, live and work with, I grow in my self-understanding and acceptance of life as it is. I come to understand my gifts and my brokenness; my strengths and my weaknesses. I come to see the Creator as the source of all life. I come to appreciate the fact and many ways in which the Creator shares His life and blessings with all peoples and all creation. I come to see that my life and all life will one day return to the Creator. As I journey in life, I see how the beauty of all creation speaks to me and others of the Beauty of the Creator.[2]

Let us visualize a native community in the course of daily events. We experience the sacredness of life, of persons—especially for little children and for our elders—of teachers. Through them, we learn the sense of the sacred, respect for our Creator, respect for one another, and respect for all creation. We also learn our ways: of sharing, of hospitality, of generosity, and of being "present" to one another. It is through our interactions and interpersonal relationships that our giftedness as native peoples comes to birth and grows within ourselves, our family, our community, our nation, and our tribe. By our intratribal experiences and learning situations, we come to a greater awareness and appreciation of our creation truths.

> By understanding my traditional values and ways of walking with the Creator, I come to appreciate the gifts and sacred ways He shares

---

2. *The Story and Faith Journey of Seventeen Native Catechists* (Great Falls, Mont.: Tekakwitha Conference, 1983), p. 84.

with me, my family, my tribe and the world. By the stories and memories of my family and my tribe, I came to learn and to respect my tribal traditions, my own giftedness and my Indianness.[3]

To continue, let us center ourselves on *time*—that time of events, of waiting, of silence, of reflection, of contemplation, of timelessness. Think of the valuable moment or moments we can spend by observing and learning from a sacred animal, bird, or insect. They teach us ways in which we can live fuller lives as human beings. The times we stand in prayer and wait to greet a new sunrise, a new day, and to give thanks for breath and for all the gifts of life. The days, weeks, and months, we wait for our crops to grow and ripen—gifts from Mother Earth. Again, the time we take to care for and watch a child grow from infancy to puberty, then into adulthood is a wonderful gift. The hours we spend to support and to pray with a family and family members who are seriously ill; the time "to be with"; to be in silence; to pray; to meditate on the new life experience of a deceased loved one as we keep vigil are all gifts. Through the many events of our lives, we learn about our Creator, about life, about creation, contemplation, silence, and patience. In effect, it is through the life within a community that one learns to believe and to experience the depth and sacredness of life, given as a gift by our Creator. Thus, faith is lived and gifted through our relationships. To really experience life is to be in harmony with our God and one another, with our extended family and our community, with nature and the whole of creation. In rhythm with the harmonious beat of our faith life, we celebrate life and gift through the elders—our storytellers and teachers—in our legends, songs, dances, and art; in and through our religious festivals and sacred ceremonies, whether on a mountain, near water, before a tree, in a desert, on a plain, in a sweat lodge, or in a gathering room, all speak of the sacredness of persons, symbols, and places.

Our elders tell us of the journeys of our people and how God has loved us and has been with us from the beginning and is still present in our own lives, in the lives of our people, and in our world. Our legends teach us about life and about making choices that help us lead a fuller life, a life of greater harmony.

We continue to express gratitude for life in the steady beat of the drum and the oneness of heart as we sing our chants during our solemn religious ceremonies and rituals or during intertribal social gatherings. For instance, our Round Dances symbolize the joy and love of being in union with our Creator and with one another and gratitude for the many gifts shared throughout the cycle of life. So too, our Honor Dances acknowledge the giftedness of our people and, in particular, our women who are respected as the life-givers for the tribe. Also, many of our dances are in recognition

---

3. Ibid.

of God's creatures and are so named to show our respect for animals and birds. For example, beauty, power, and strength are shown in the Eagle Dance. Some of our dances tell a story about the life expeditions and events of our people, such as in the Canoe Dance, which is a journey; and, then, that eventful time of life—mating as expressed in the Partridge Dance.

Our many rituals, using significant gestures and symbols, bring us in closer union with our Creator, who made us and loved us from all time, and who is giver of all good things and continues to love and bless us each day. In response, we give praise and thanksgiving for a new day as we offer ourselves, our cedar in the four directions. At the same time, we recall our own brokenness and need for healing as we purify, cleanse, and bless ourselves with smoking sweetgrass and water—a continual reminder of who we are before the Creator.

As we experience the various events and stages in our lives, our naming ceremonies help us to identify ourselves as individuals and as members of a family. Furthermore, some rituals, in various tribes, initiate members into another stage of human growth and development through prayer, fasting, and physical pain—truly a spiritual and religious experience of one's whole being. These rituals of human growth might take shape as the sun dance, a puberty rite, or a vision quest. Moreover, a person's fullness of earthly life is celebrated with deep faith and hope that the spirit is on a journey to a much fuller life, as the community gathers to share in the joy at the beginning of a new life by all-night vigils, prayer, dances, games, feasting, and give-aways. In effect, it is in all events of our cyclic life that we breathe the fullness of God's revelation to us native people. Consequently, gospel values are lived experiences in our way of life.[4]

In an insightful and sensitive article, "A Cross-Cultural Approach to Catechesis among Native Americans," Gilbert Hemauer, OFM Cap., stated that "the urgent need exists to recognize the 'good news' native American people and culture already possess in their rich traditions and ways of living."[5] It is important to bear in mind that an "arduous and deliberate process of incarnational catechesis is slow, gradual and must be freely chosen."[6]

As a result of Fr. Hemauer's concern for ongoing faith development and for setting some catechetical foundations for native peoples so that "the word be made flesh," he convened and facilitated a four-day sharing

---

4. National Conference of Catholic Bishops, *Statement of U.S. Catholic Bishops on American Indians* (Washington, D.C.: USCC Office of Publishing and Promotion Services, 1977), p. 3.

5. Gilbert F. Hemauer, "A Cross-Cultural Approach to Catechesis among Native Americans," *The Living Light* 14:1(Spring 1977): 132–137.

6. Ibid., p. 137.

with seventeen native catechists. The November 1982 meeting on native catechesis development was held in Denver, Colorado. Sr. Mariella Frye, MHSH, USCC representative for catechetical ministry, was invited to guide the group in the consultation process.

As one of the seventeen catechists, I found it to be a time of rich, spiritual experiences of prayer. It was a time of openness to one another; a time to share hurts and feelings, sorrows and joys, tears and laughter; a time to learn one another's tribal histories, traditions, and customs. Frequently, I found myself asking the same question that Jesus asked his disciples: "Who do you say that I am?" (Mt 16:15).

As we progressed through the process, we learned how each of us has walked with the Lord—either alone, with our family, with our native community, or with others who have helped us become who we are today. We recalled the numerous occasions when we felt Jesus' healing power and were healed from past wounds of prejudice, injustice, and mockery. In remembering the times Jesus was with us, we were able to face difficult situations. We were strengthened by many joy-filled events that were life-giving because we experienced His presence, love, and peace through each other as we were being called into a deeper love and faith. We could exclaim with Simon Peter, "You are the Messiah, the Son of the Living God" (Mt 16:16).

As the days continued, the seventeen of us were no longer strangers but brothers and sisters—sacraments to one another. Definitely, a small community of faith was formed with love and trust. We were able to discover and rediscover, affirm and reaffirm, our own giftedness as the Creator's loved ones touched by his gentleness and presence.

We further explored and meditated on our faith, our gift of Catholicism. We came to a much more profound awareness and expression of who we are as native Catholics. We felt the powerful presence of Jesus in the sacraments of the Catholic Church. We remembered how we have experienced and been touched by Jesus' sacramental presence in our lives and how we have been changed, transformed, when we opened ourselves in God's revelation in our lives.

As the hours of retelling came to a close, we developed a tentative framework for developing a native catechesis under three main clarifications: (1) discovery of one's personal truth as learned and reenforced by our parents, grandparents, aunts, and uncles; (2) appreciation of our creation truths as we have listened to our legends and tribal stories; (3) our experience of Jesus as we listened to and meditated on his word and shared Jesus in our lives through relationships and the sacraments.

Further native catechesis development can be found in a basic, four-course outline drawn up in July 1985 by Sr. Genevieve Cuny, OSF (Oglala Sioux), Fr. Michael Galvan (Ohlone), and myself, Sr. Kateri Mitchell, SSA (Mohawk), coordinator of the summer catechesis programs, under the auspices of the Tekakwitha Conference National Center, Great Falls,

Montana. These courses are offered to assist native and nonnative catechists in bringing a deeper and richer understanding of the gospel message
and values to the lives of our people. In such a manner, we teach as Jesus
did through our relationships with God, creation, our family, nature,
Mother Earth, and the gifts of our tribal traditions, customs, and rituals.

In the following outlines, the purpose is to provide a process that will
aid our people to help one another live in harmony with God, our Creator,
with self, with one another, and with all creation in light of the "good
news."

Catechesis I is a personal faith journey that considers three main areas:
first, a discovery of one's personal truth as a native, as a Christian; second,
focus on an appreciation of our creation truths, both in the tribe and in
sacred Scripture; third, our experience of Jesus as Catholics called to know,
love, and serve.

Catechesis I
Personal Faith Journey

 I. Discovery of One's Personal Truth
    Accept
    A. reality of sin and grace (life as it is)
    B. acceptance of individual creation truths (personal faith journey)
    C. traditional ways
    D. Christian ways
    Respond
    A. using gifts (individual and traditional)
    B. our loving Creator (You who have many names) shares his love,
       breathes his life, tells his truth
 II. Appreciation of our Creation Truths
    A. His creation truth as told by my people (elders, grandparents)
    B. His truth of creation as told in his sacred Word (Old Testament)
    C. other peoples' creation truth
III. Our Experience of Jesus
    A. Catholic Church's experience of Jesus (evangelization)
    B. how I come to know Jesus (message)
    C. how I come to love Jesus (community building and worship)
    D. how I come to serve Jesus (service)

Catechesis II covers the areas and stages of human growth and faith
development focusing both on the native and Christian ways and how we
interact with other cultures.

Catechesis II
Faith Development

  I. Human Growth and Development
 II. Native American Development Values
III. Stages of Faith
 IV. Communication Skills in Christian Perspective
  V. Developing Sensitivities and Understanding between Cultures in Sharing Faith

Catechesis III explores the sacramental life and God's plan for salvation through the presence of the risen Lord in the sacraments and through the sacred actions of all tribes by their values, rites, ceremonies, and celebrations.

Catechesis III
Sacraments

  I. God Becomes Man for Us
 II. The Spirit Brings Salvation to Us
III. The Presence of the Risen Lord
 IV. The Sacraments: Jesus Promises To Be with His Disciples
  V. God Works through the Sacred Actions of All Tribes
      A. rites and ceremonies: naming ceremonies, sweat lodge, medicine men, elders, vision quest, puberty rites, sun dance, purification
      B. values and celebrations: birth, marriage, death, hospitality, generosity, respect for life, land

Catechesis IV calls forth creative ways to share the Christian message within a cultural context and to develop native catechetical materials relevant to the different tribes.

Catechesis IV
Aproaches in Native Catechesis

  I. Called To Be Creative in Relating Culture and Christian Message
 II. Shared Christian Praxis Approach (Broome)
III. Developing Materials
      A. *Family Cluster Model* (Sr. Genevieve Cuny—article available through the Tekakwitha Conference National Center, Great Falls, Montana)
      B. *Finding A Way Home* (Fr. Pat Twohy, SJ, Seattle University, Broadway and Madison, Seattle, WA 98122; University Press, Spokane, WA 99220)

C. *Labre Pilot Religious Ed Project* (Ashland, MT)

D. *Builders of the New Earth*, volumes I, II, III (Fr. John Hatcher, Box 271, Plainview, SD 57748; (605) 985-5906; and Fr. Pat McCorkell, published by the Diocese of Rapid City)

E. *Dakota Way of Life* (Palm)

To enhance the program, the Tekakwitha Center presently serves as a hub and is collecting and encouraging further development of materials by our native people that can be shared and distributed to the conference membership as needs and requests arise. Also, to date, the national center has hired a full-time director of communications, Mr. Cy Peck, Jr. (Tlingit), who is providing a collection of audiovisuals of numerous tribal events and varied workshops held in Great Falls, which are valuable resources available through the Conference to help lead our people toward greater self-awareness and wholeness.

As we continue to move forward, one of our primary program goals is to engage full time a native person to develop native catechetical materials and to provide ongoing native catechesis program coordination and program development so as to serve more effectively and to share the gospel message and values of Jesus more meaningfully with our native communities.

In conclusion, we can agree with Sr. Mariella Frye when she states that catechesis ". . . is sharing one's faith by proclaiming the entire Christian message; forming a community of believers; helping people to pray and to worship; and motivating them to serve others."[7]

---

7. *The Story and Faith Journey of Seventeen Native Catechists*, p. 84

IV. RESOURCES

**Resources for the
Southeast Asian Community**

**Resources for
the Black Community**

**Resources for
the Hispanic Community**

**Resources for
the Native American Community**

**Selected Bibliography for
Intercultural and Interracial
Relations**

Resources for the Southeast Asian Community

Books/Publications

National Conference of Catholic Bishops. *Resolution on the Pastoral Concern of the Church for People on the Move.* Washington, D.C.: USCC Office of Publishing and Promotion Services, 1976.

_____. *Together, A New People: Pastoral Statement on Migrants and Refugees.* Washington, D.C.: USCC Office of Publishing and Promotion Services, 1987.

Pastoral Care of Migrants and Refugees. *Introduction to Filipino Ministry.* Washington, D.C.: Pastoral Care of Migrants and Refugees (PCMR).

_____. *Pastoral Care of Migrants and Refugees Brochure.* Washington, D.C.: PCMR.

_____. *Pastoral Care of Migrants and Refugees Newsletter.* Washington, D.C.: PCMR.

_____. *Proceedings of the First Meeting of the Cambodian, Hmong, and Laotian Apostolate in the Catholic Church in the United States.* Washington, D.C.: PCMR.

_____. *Proceedings of the 1986 Meeting of the Cambodian, Hmong, and Laotian Apostolate.* Washington, D.C.: PCMR.

Cambodian Religious Literature

Approaches to the Khmer Mentality. Washington, D.C.: PCMR.

Cambodian Song Book. Washington, D.C.: PCMR.

Cambodian Sunday Missal. Washington, D.C.: PCMR.

CHIVIT THMEY (New Life) Cambodian-language newsletter. Washington, D.C.: PCMR.

Khmer New Testament. Washington, D.C.: PCMR.

Khmer Psalm Book. Washington, D.C.: PCMR.

Let Us Listen to the Word of God: Guidelines to Help Cambodian Catechumens. Washington, D.C.: PCMR.

Hmong Religious Literature

First Steps in Hmong. St. Paul: Church of Saint Mary.

Funeral Song in Hmong. St. Paul: Church of Saint Mary.

The Gospel: Our Life and Our Happiness. St. Paul: Church of Saint Mary.

Hmong Bible. St. Paul: Church of Saint Mary.

Hmong/English Catechism. Fresno: The Asian Ministry Office.

Hmong/English Missalette. St. Paul: Church of Saint Mary.

Regular Letters. St. Paul: Church of Saint Mary.

Tsimneej Tshiab. St. Paul: Church of Saint Mary.

Laotian Religious Literature

Baptism of Infants; Baptism of Adults; Marriage; Annointing of the Sick. Booklets. Fort Worth: Laotian Pastoral Center.

Desa Phranam Phrabida: Catechisme Catholique Laotien. Chicago: St. Michael's Church.

Laotian/English Catechism. Fort Worth: Laotian Pastoral Center.

Missals, Hymns, Catechisms, and the New Testament, Part II. Stockton, Calif.: St. Luke's Church.

New Life: Laotian Music Book. Chicago: St. Michael's Church.

Phavana. Fort Worth: Laotian Pastoral Center.

Phra Vorasan khong Phra Jesu Chao (The Gospel). Fort Worth: Laotian Pastoral Center.

Sadudee: Laotian Song Book. Chicago: St. Michael's Church.

SENG ARUN. Fort Worth: Laotian Pastoral Center.

Vietnamese Religious Materials

Catholic News Magazine; Bible; Missal; Catechism; and *Prayer Books.* Mountain View, Calif.: St. Patrick's College.

Bible; Missal; Old and New Catechism. San Jose: Vietnamese Pastoral Center.

Audiocassettes

Laotian Liturgical Music Tape. Chicago: St. Michael's Church.

Tapes and Booklet about the Prayers and Songs in Hmong. St. Paul: Church of Saint Mary.

Tapes in Hmong To Teach Hmong Catechumens. St. Paul: Church of Saint Mary.

Organizations

Pastoral Care of Migrants and Refugees (PCMR). The office within the National Conference of Catholic Bishops that was established to care for the spiritual needs of refugees and immigrants living in the United States. One of the functions this office serves is as a central resource library for bilingual and ethnic religious materials. For more information contact:

Pastoral Care of Migrants and Refugees
National Conference of Catholic Bishops
1312 Massachusetts Avenue, N.W.
Washington, DC 20005
(202) 659-6681

Resources for the Black Community

Books/Publications

Black American Bishops. *What We Have Seen and Heard: A Pastoral Letter on Evangelization*. Cincinnati: St. Anthony Messenger Press, 1984.

Bowman, Sr. Thea, ed. *Families: Black and Catholic, Catholic and Black*. Washington, D.C.: USCC Office of Publishing and Promotion Services, 1985.

Faith Journey Series. Supplementary Christian education series for grade 5 through adult. Biblically based, with illustrative stories drawn from black history and contemporary experience. New York: United Church Press, 1986.

Jones, Nathan. *Sharing the Old, Old Story: Educational Ministry in the Black Community*. Minnesota: St. Mary's Press, 1983.

Kunjufu, Jawanza. *Developing Positive Self-Images and Discipline in Black Children*. Chicago: Afro-Am Publishing Co., 1984.

The National Black Sisters' Conference. *Tell It Like It Is: A Black Catholic Perspective on Christian Education*. Oklahoma: The National Black Sisters' Conference (NBSC), 1983.

Journals/Periodicals

Pass It On. Bimonthly newsletter for persons engaged in pastoral/educational ministries in black communities. Chicago: Ethnic Communications Outlet, 1986.

Institutes/Organizations

Council on Interracial Books for Children
1841 Broadway
New York, NY 10023
(212) 757-5339

Ethnic Communications Outlet
4107 West 26th Street
Chicago, IL 60615
(312) 522-5151

The Imani Program
2203 Second Street
New Orleans, LA 70113
(504) 895-7749 or (504) 522-8843
Contact: Sr. Addie Walker

Institute for Black Catholic Studies
934 South Cortez
New Orleans, LA 70125
(314) 531-4506
Contact: Rev. Thaddeus Posey

Josephite Pastoral Center
1200 Varnum Street, N.E.
Washington, DC 20017
(202) 526-9270

Resources for the Hispanic Community

Books/Publications

De la Cruz, María and Francis J. Buckley. *Fey Cultura*. Ramsey, N.J.: Paulist Press, 1986.

Erevia, Angela. *Quince Años: Celebrando una Tradición*. Bilingual catechetical material directed to young people, particularly those of Hispanic origin. San Antonio, Tex.: Missionary Catechists of Divine Providence, 1985.

González, O.R. and M. La Velle. *The Hispanic Catholic in the United States: A Sociocultural and Religious Profile*. New York: Northeast Catholic Pastoral Center for Hispanics, 1985.

Hall, Suzanne. "The Hispanic Presence: Implications for Catholic Education" in *Momentum*, Journal of the National Catholic Educational Association (February 1986): 43–45.

Herrera, Marina. *Adult Religious Education for the Hispanic Community*. Washington, D.C.: The National Conference of Diocesan Directors of Religious Education, 1984.

Ivory, Thomas. *Creciendo en Fe con su Niño (Growing in Faith with Your Child)*. Iowa: William C. Brown, 1978.

Merrill, Harmin. *Yo Soy Así, Cuaderno de Trabajo*. Illinois: Developmental Learning Materials, 1976.

National Federation for Catholic Youth Ministry. *El Reto de la Catequesis de Adolescentes: Madurez en la Fe (The Challenge of Adolescent Catechesis: Maturity in Faith)*. Washington, D.C.: The National Federation for Catholic Youth Ministry, 1986.

USCC Department of Education. *Domingo Catequístico de 1986: Proclama La Verdad con Amor (Proclaim the Truth with Love)*. Washington, D.C.: USCC Office of Publishing and Promotion Services, 1986.

_____. *Metodología y Temas para una Catequésis Hispana (Methodology and Themes for Hispanic Catechesis)*. Washington, D.C.: United States Catholic Conference, 1979.

_____. *Visión para el Ministerio con Jóvenes (A Vision of Youth Ministry)*. Washington, D.C.: USCC Office of Publishing and Promotion Services, 1986.

USCC/NCCB Secretariat for Hispanic Affairs/Department of Education. *En Marcha Hacia el Señor (Journeying Together toward the Lord)*. Catechetical materials for use with Hispanic migrant workers. Washington, D.C.: USCC Office of Publishing and Promotion Services, 1982.

Catechetical Resource Contacts

Ms. Carmen Cervantes
Office of Religious Education
1125 N. Lincoln Street
Stockton, CA 95204
(209) 466-6796

Sr. Angela Erevia, MCDP
Office of Religious Education
P.O. Box 4708
Victoria, TX 77903
(512) 573-0828

Dr. María de los Angeles García
Office of Religious Education
269 Oliver Street
Newark, NJ 07105
(201) 596-3991

Sr. Rose Monique Peña, OP
Office of Religious Education
9401 Biscayne Boulevard
Miami Shores, FL 33138
(305) 757-6241

Sr. María Tránsito Sánchez, CACH
Catechetical Office
1011 First Avenue
New York, NY 10022
(212) 371-1000

Sr. Maruja Sedano, SAC
Office of Religious Education
1520 West Ninth Street
Los Angeles, CA 90015
(213) 251-3349

Ms. María Pilar La Torre
Office of Religious Education
1 Lake Street
Brighton, MA 02135
(617) 254-4425

Sr. María de Jesus Ybarra, OP
Office of Religious Education
408 West Chestnut Avenue
Yakima, WA 98902
(509) 248-1910

Institutes/Organizations

Hispanic Research Center
Fordham University
Bronx, NY 10458

Instituto de Liturgia Hispana
540 N.W. 132nd Street
North Miami, FL 33168
(305) 681-7428
Contact: Rev. Juan Sosa

The Leaven Movement *(El Movimiento Levadura)*
Sisters of Mercy of the Union
1320 Fenwick Lane, Suite 610
Silver Spring, MD 20910.

Mexican American Cultural Center
3019 W. French Place
San Antonio, TX 78284
(512) 732-2156

Midwest Institute for Hispanic Ministry
P.O. Box 703
Notre Dame, IN 46556
Contact: Ms. Olga Villa

National Office of RENEW
Archdiocese of Newark
269 Oliver Street
Newark, NJ 07105
(201) 769-5400
Contact: Rev. Thomas Dowd

Northeast Pastoral Institute
1011 First Avenue
New York, NY 10022
(212) 751-7045
Contact: Rev. Roberto Gonzalez

Southeast Pastoral Institute
2900 S.W. 87th Avenue
Miami, FL 33165
(305) 223-7711
Contact: Sr. Soledad Galeon, RMI

Resources for the Native American Community

Books/Publications

Henry, Jeanette and Rupert Costo. *A Thousand Years of American Indian Storytelling*. San Francisco: The Indian Historian Press, 1976.

National Conference of Catholic Bishops. *Statement of U.S. Catholic Bishops on American Indians*. Washington, D.C.: Office of Publishing and Promotion Services, 1977.

Starkloff, Carl, SJ. *People of the Center*. New York: Seabury Press, 1974.

Steltenkamp, Michael. *The Sacred Vision*. Ramsey, N.J.: Paulist Press, 1982.

Stolzman, William, SJ. *The Pipe and Christ*. Chamberlain, S.Dak.: St. Joseph's Indian School, 1986.

Tekakwitha Conference. *The Story and Faith Journey of Seventeen Native Catechists*. A consultation in native catechesis. Great Falls, Mont.: Tekakwitha Conference National Center, 1982.

Tooker, Elisabeth, ed. *Native North American Spirituality of the Eastern Woodlands*. Ramsey, N.J.: Paulist Press, 1979.

Twohy, Patrick J. *Finding A Way Home*. Spokane: University Press, 1983.

Weatherford, Elizabeth and Emilia Seubert, eds. *Native Americans on Film and Video*. New York: Museum of the American Indian, 1981.

Zeilinger, Ron. *Lakota Life*. An exchange of Lakota and Christian ideas in the spirit of the U.S. Catholic Bishops' 1977 *Statement on Native Americans*, 1984.

Film/Videocassettes

Another Face of Jesus. (Filmstrip and Cassette). American Indian artist Dick West has painted a series of pictures depicting Jesus as an American Indian, thus adding to the world's interpretations of Jesus as the Savior of all people. Interspersed throughout the filmstrip are pictures of some of Dr. West's wood sculptures and others of his paintings of Indian life done in oils, water color, and tempera. Helpful in presenting another cultural picture. Valley Forge: American Baptist Films.

An Indian Jesus. (Script and Guide). Selected paintings from the filmstrip *Another Face of Jesus* are used to help children see Jesus from the point of view of an American Indian. Artist Dick West, a Cheyenne Indian, uses vibrant colors and his knowledge of Indian culture to make events from the life of Jesus come alive with meaning.

Brebeuf's Dream. (Video). Ministry Among Canadian Native American Deacons.

Journey of Hope. (Video). 1985 Documentary on the Tekakwitha Conference, telling its history and how it is empowering the people to develop a truly native Catholic Church.

Pilgrim in Huronia. (Video). Pope John Paul II's 1984 visit to Native Americans in Canada.

The Good Mind. (Video). An examination of some of the beliefs of Christianity and beliefs of traditional native Americans. Nashville: United Methodist Publishing House.

Additional Resources

The following are gatherings of native people to celebrate tribal and Catholic traditions: Annual Tekakwitha Conference; Local Mini-Tekakwitha Conference; Regional Tekakwitha Conference; Parish Tekakwitha Circles and Clubs; Catholic Indian Congresses; Pow Wows; Intertribal Sharings.

The following are some of the resource people who offer guidance to native Americans: Tribal Members; Medicine People; Holy People; Permanent Deacons; Spiritual Teachers, who inspire us in the journey of life.

Institutes/Organizations

Anishnabe Spiritual Center
Anderson Lake
Espanola, Ontario
Canada, P0P IC0

Bureau of Catholic Indian Missions
2021 H Street N.W.
Washington, DC 20006

The Indian Historical Society
1451 Masonic Avenue
San Francisco, CA 94117

Institute on Pluralism and Group Identity
165 East 56th Street
New York, NY 10022

Kisemanito Centre
Grouard, Alberta
Canada, T0G IC0

Museum of the American Indian
Broadway at 155th Street
New York, NY 10032

Sioux Spiritual Center
Howes Star Route
Box 271
Plainview, SD 57748

Tekakwitha Conference National Center
P.O. Box 6759
Great Falls, MT 59406-6759

Selected Bibliography for Intercultural and Interracial Relations

Books/Publications

Aliport, Gordon W. *The Nature of Prejudice.* Garden City, N.Y.: Doubleday & Co., Inc., 1954.

Banks, James A. *Teaching Strategies for Ethnic Studies.* Boston: Allyn and Bacon, 1975.

Blubaugh, Jon A. and Dorothy L. Pennington. *Crossing Differences: Interracial Communication.* Columbus, Ohio: Charles E. Merrill Publishing, Co., 1976.

Burger, Henry G. *Ethno-Pedagogy: A Manual in Cultural Sensitivity, with Techniques for Improving Cross-Cultural Teaching by Fitting Ethnic Patterns.* Albuquerque, N.M.: Southwestern Cooperative Educational Laboratory, 1971.

Casse, Pierre. *Training for the Cross-Cultural Mind: A Handbook for Cross-Cultural Trainers and Consultants.* Washington, D.C.: The Society for Intercultural Education, Training and Research, 1980.

Condon, John C. *Interacts: Mexicans and North Americans,* Chicago: Intercultural Press, 1980.

Darrow, Kenneth and Bradley Palmquist. *The Transcultural Study Guide.* Palo Alto, Calif.: Volunteers in Asia, 1975.

Eisman, Edward. *UNITAS: Building Healing Communities for Children: A Developmental Training Manual.* New York Hispanic Research Center, Fordham University, 1982.

Fantini, Marion D. and R. Cardenas. *Parenting in a Multicultural Society.* Linigman Publishing Co., 1980.

Flannery, Austin, OP, ed. "Decree on the Church's Missionary Activity" in *Vatican Council II: The Conciliar and Post Conciliar Documents.* Collegeville, Minn.: The Liturgical Press, 1975.

_____. "Pastoral Constitution on the Church in the Modern World" in *Vatican Council II: Conciliar and Post Conciliar Documents.* Collegeville, Minn.: The Liturgical Press, 1975.

Gold, Milton J., Carl A. Grant and Harry N. Rivlin, eds. *In Praise of Diversity: A Resource Book for Multicultural Education.* Washington, D.C.: Teacher Corps, Association of Teacher Educators, 1977.

Gudykunst, William B. and Young Yun Kim. *Communicating with Strangers: An Approach to Intercultural Communication.* Reading, Mass.: Addison-Wesley Publishing, Co., 1984.

Hall, Edward. *The Silent Language.* Garden City, N.Y.: Anchor Press, 1963.

_____. The Hidden Dimension. Garden City, N.Y.: Doubleday & Co., Inc., 1966.

_____. *Beyond Culture.* Garden City, N.Y.: Anchor Press, 1976.

Hater, Rev. Robert J. *Parish Catechetical Ministry.* Resource of the National Conference of Diocesan Directors of Religious Education. Encino, Calif.: Glencoe Publishing Co., 1986.

Herrera, Marina. "Toward Multicultural Youth Ministry," *Readings in Youth Ministry Volume I: Foundations.* Washington, D.C.: National Federation for Catholic Youth Ministry, 1986.

_____. *LASER: Creating Unity in Diversity.* Washington, D.C.: National Catholic Conference for International Justice, 1985.

John Paul II. *On Catechesis in Our Time.* Apostolic Exhortation *Catechesi Tradendae.* Washington, D.C.: USCC Office of Publishing and Promotion Services, 1979.

Kohls, Robert L. *Developing Intercultural Awareness: A Learning Module Complete with Lesson Plan, Content, Exercise and Handouts.* Washington, D.C.: The Society for Intercultural Education, Training and Research, 1981.

Levin, Jack. *The Functions of Prejudice.* New York: Harper & Row Publications, 1975.

National Conference of Catholic Bishops. *Brothers and Sisters to Us.* Pastoral Letter on Racism in Our Day. Washington, D.C.: USCC Office of Publishing and Promotion Services, 1979.

——————————. *Cultural Pluralism in the United States.* Washington, D.C.: USCC Office of Publishing and Promotion Services, 1980.

——————————. *The Hispanic Presence: Challenge and Commitment.* Pastoral Letter on Hispanic Ministry. Washington, D.C.: USCC Office of Publishing and Promotion Services, 1983.

——————————. *Statement of U.S. Catholic Bishops on American Indians.* Washington, D.C.: USCC Office of Publishing and Promotion Services, 1977.

——————————. *To Teach as Jesus Did.* Pastoral Message on Catholic Education. Washington, D.C.: USCC Office of Publishing and Promotion Services, 1973.

Padilla, Amado M., ed. *Acculturation: Theory, Models and Some New Findings.* Denver, Colo.: American Association for the Advancement of Science, 1980.

Papajohn, and J. Spiegel. *Transactions in Families.* San Francisco, Washington, D.C., London: Jossey-Bass Publishers, 1975.

Paul VI. *Evangelization in the Modern World.* Washington, D.C.: USCC Office of Publishing and Promotion Services, 1976.

Pelaez, Armantina. *The Multicultural Dimension of Young Adult Ministry.* Naugatuck, Conn.: Center for Youth Ministry Department, 1987.

Powell, Philip Wayne. *Tree of Hate.* New York/London: Basic Books, Inc., 1971.

The Presbyterian Center. *Racial Ethnic Faith Journeys.* (From Kindergarden to Adult—A two-year cycle with three levels). Atlanta: Genieve Press, 1983.

Pusch, Margaret D. *Multicultural Education: A Cross-Cultural Training Approach*. Chicago, Ill.: Intercultural Network, Inc., 1979.

Ries, Peter. *Catechesis in Formation*. Book One. Encino, Calif.: Benziger Publishing Co., 1984.

Sacred Congregation for the Clergy. *General Catechetical Directory*. Washington, D.C.: USCC Office of Publishing and Promotion Services, 1971.

Samovar, Larry A. and Richard E. Porter, eds. *Intercultural Communication: A Reader*. Belmont, Calif.: Wadsworth Publishing, Co., Inc., 1976.

Secretariat of Ethnic and Cultural Affairs. *Light of Nations: Ministry to Ethnic Groups*. Archdiocese of San Francisco, 1985.

Stewart, Edward C. *American Cultural Patterns: A Cross-Cultural Perspective*. Washington, D.C.: The Society for Intercultural Education Training and Research, 1972.

USCC Department of Education. *Sharing the Light of Faith*. National Catechetical Directory for Catholics in the United States. Washington, D.C.: USCC Office of Publishing and Promotion Services, 1979.

_____. *Sharing the Light of Faith: An Official Commentary*. Washington, D.C.: USCC Office of Publishing and Promotion Services, 1981.

_____. *Families: Black and Catholic, Catholic and Black*. Washington, D.C.: Office of Publishing and Promotion Services, 1985.

USCC Office of Pastoral Care of Migrants and Refugees. *Pastoral Care of Migrants and Refugees Directory*. Washington, D.C.: USCC Office of Publishing and Promotion Services, 1987.

USCC Secretariat for Hispanic Affairs. *Prophetic Voices*. The Document on the Process of the III Encuentro Nacional Hispano de Pastoral. USCC Office of Publishing and Promotion Services, 1987.

Wall, Muriel. *Directory of Intercultural Education Newsletters.* Information Consulting Associates, 303 W. Pleasantview Ave., Hackensack, NJ 07601.

Articles/Periodicals

Hemauer, Rev. Gilbert F. "A Cross-Cultural Approach to Catechesis among Native Americans" in *The Living Light,* vol. 14, no. 1 (Spring 1977): 132–137.

Herrera, Marina. "Sharing Scripture with the Non-Print Oriented" in *Liturgy,* vol. 2, no. 3, 1982.

——————. "Communicating the Faith in a Multicultural Society" in *Catechist* (September 1983).

Lindsay, Austin. "The Challenge of the Multicultural Parish" in *Today's Parish,* (October 1982).

——————. "Popular Spirituality" in *Today's Parish,* (September 1983).

——————. "The Multicultural Church and Evangelization" in *Emmanuel,* vol. 87, no. 11 (December 1981).

Mindel, H. Charles. "Extended Familism Among Urban Mexican Americans, Anglos and Blacks" in *Hispanic Journal of Behavioral Science,* vol. 2, no. 1 (1980): 21–34.

Sluzki, C.E. "Migration and Family Conflict" in *Family Process,* vol. 18, 379–390.

Wakil, P.S., M.C. Siddique and F. Wakil. "Between Two Cultures: A Study of Socialization of Children Immigrants" in *Journal of Marriage and Family Therapy,* vol. 43, (November 1981): 929–940.

About the Authors

 **Sr. María de la Cruz Aymes, SH,** was born of French parents in Mexico and joined the Society of Helpers in the United States. During her religious formation, she worked with Puerto Ricans in New York, blacks in San Francisco, war-torn children in France, and poor villages in her native Mexico. For the last thirty years, she has labored in the catechetical field in the United States. She has authored the original ON OUR WAY series, which served as a model for many other religion textbooks and co-authored the NEW LIFE, LORD OF LIFE, and GOD WITH US programs published by Sadlier. She has lectured extensively throughout the United States, Latin America, the Orient and Australia. She is a member of the International Catechetical Council of.the Sacred Congregation for the Clergy. Her multicultural experience led her recently to write FE Y CULTURA (Paulist Press) for the formation of Hispanic catechists.

 **Sr. Genevieve Cuny, OSF,** is an Oglala Sioux Franciscan who was born and raised on the Pine Ridge Indian Reservation in South Dakota. She has a BS in Education from Regis College, Denver; an MA in Business Education from the University of Detroit, Michigan; and an MA in Religious Education from Loyola University, Chicago. For the past twenty years, she has served the Indian people on the Rosebud and Pine Ridge Reservations in South Dakota in religious education and pastoral ministry. Presently, she is coordinator of the newly established Office of native American Catechetics in the Diocese of Rapid City. She is active in the Tekakwitha Conference, a national Catholic voice for native Americans in the United States and Canada and spends six weeks each summer at its national headquarters in Great Falls, Montana, giving workshops in native catechetics and developing native American catechetical materials.

 **Toinette M. Eugene, Ph.D.,** is Associate Professor of Education, Society, and Black Church Studies at Colgate Rochester Divinity School in Rochester, New York, where she teaches pastoral theology. Dr. Eugene's primary academic expertise and research interests center on religious education and ecclesiology in the black community and on feminist issues in Church and society. She has published numerous articles on the integration of spirituality and social justice as essential to meet the challenges of ministry in educational and cultural settings. Dr. Eugene is currently serving as a consultant to the United States Catholic bishops, who are drafting a national pastoral letter in response to women's concerns.

 **Rev. Michael Galvan,** a member of the Ohlone tribe, is a priest of the Roman Catholic Diocese of Oakland. He has an MA in Christian Ethics and an STL in Christian Spirituality. He is a Ph.D. candidate in Christian Spirituality at the Graduate Theological Union in Berkeley, California. Father Galvan serves as the Director of Clergy Formation for the Diocese of Oakland. He is also part of the faculty for the Tekakwitha Summer Programs and works with the Tekakwitha Conference's task forces on catechetics and ministry.

 **María Luisa Gastón** is a single, lay Catholic, born in Havana, Cuba, with an MA in Religious Studies from The Catholic University of America. Since 1981, she has served as Executive Secretary of the Southeast Pastoral Institute (SEPI), where she is also a professor and member of the SE Regional Pastoral Team. Ms. Gaston has experience in planning and facilitating local and national programs for Hispanic leadership and is a member of the National Facilitators Team of the III Encuentro Nacional Hispano. Her previous experience includes working with the NCCB/USCC Secretariat for Hispanic Affairs in Washington, D.C., as well as Hispanic ministry in Baltimore, Maryland and Waukesha, Wisconsin.

 **Marina Herrera, Ph.D.,** is a specialist in multicultural catechesis. She writes, offers workshops, and assists dioceses, parishes, seminaries, and schools in the development of multicultural religious education programs. She lectures at the Washington Theological Union. Her articles appear in *Catechist, The Religious Education Journal, Liturgy, Momentum,* and *PACE.*

Nathan Jones, Ph.D., is Religious Education Coordinator for Englewood School, a cluster of six Catholic elementary schools on Chicago's South Side, as well as Editor for Ethnic Communications Outlet, Chicago. He comes to his work with experience in urban pastoral ministry and diocesan administration and is a regular columnist with *Catechist*. He is also the author of a wide range of educational resources. Dr. Jones' doctorate is in Adult Religious Education from Union Graduate School, Cincinnati.

Bishop James P. Lyke, OFM, Ph.D., is the Auxiliary Bishop of Cleveland. He was a member of the National Catechetical Directory Committee and did his doctoral paper on "A Black Perspective on the National Catechetical Directory."

Sr. Kateri Mitchell, a Mohawk from the St. Regis Indian Reservation in Hogansburg, New York, is a Sister of St. Ann. She has an MA in Education Administration and has had experience in teaching, school administration, and pastoral ministry. Presently, Sr. Kateri is a staff member at the Kisemanito Centre in Grouard, Alberta, Canada, for training native leaders in ministry. She is part of the Tekakwitha Conference National Center Summer Programs faculty for Basic Directions in Native Ministry and for Native Catechesis. Sister Kateri is also coordinator for the Tekakwitha Conference Catechetical Task Force and for the Catechesis Summer Workshops.

Rev. Umberto Nespolo, OMI, a native of Italy, is currently the Director of Ministry for the Hmong-Lao Refugees/Asian Catholic Peoples in the Diocese of Fresno, California. From 1960 to 1975, Father Nespolo served as a missionary in Laos, Southeast Asia. He has also served as Chaplain of St. Gabriel College in Thailand; Professor of French, Laotian, Art, and Music in Dao Houng, Catholic College in Laos; Founder of Dara Samouth School and Missionary for Hmong-Lao-K'Hmu peoples in North Laos Province; and Director and Missionary of Seng Savang School and Lao-Hmong-Phay peoples in Sayaboury, Laos.